# A Light in the Darkness

# A Light in the Darkness

## Lisa White

Copyright 2010 Lisa White

ISBN: 978-0-557-37399-4

# Prologue

*Please, God, let me be dead.*

I opened my eyes hoping I was somewhere else—wherever dead people go, that's where I wanted to be. A void was filling my soul like the rumbling turbulence that builds before a storm. Tears fell from my now-lifeless eyes as I silently wept.

*What's happening to me? Why will no one listen to me? Why doesn't anyone care?*

I could hear the soft, pastoral warbles of songbirds outside my window. The warm morning sun kissed my face as it peeked through the curtains.

*How can anything be pleasant? Why is the world continuing on like nothing has happened? Why do people continue to laugh? Why am I the only one feeling this? Why is God doing this to me?*

Inside, I ached with extreme anguish.

*I can't breathe. I feel so very heavy. I feel like I'm at the bottom of a hellish abyss with no way of getting out. Why won't anyone help me?*

I detested myself, and I obsessed, day and night, that I would just die, and I fantasized about all the possible ways to end my miserable life.

I couldn't bear the pain I felt inside any longer: I had to kill myself. The routine heaviness of life had exhausted me and even as simple a movement as putting one foot in front of the other was exasperating.

*Poison.*

A wave of satisfaction filled me at the thought.

*But what kind of poison can I get my hands on that will do the job?*

# Contents

**Prologue** ............................................................................................ v
**Chapter 1.**     The Power Pole ............................................................ 1
**Chapter 2.**     Meeting Mark ............................................................. 19
**Chapter 3.**     Eating Poison ............................................................. 25
**Chapter 4.**     The Hospital .............................................................. 31
**Chapter 5.**     Jaime ......................................................................... 41
**Chapter 6.**     51/50 .......................................................................... 53
**Chapter 7.**     The Gun .................................................................... 63
**Chapter 8.**     The Psychiatric Hospital ........................................... 71
**Chapter 9.**     Guardian Hospital ..................................................... 97
**Chapter 10.**   The Warrior Within ................................................. 109
**Epilogue** ...................................................................................... 113

# Chapter 1

## The Power Pole

The mild spring night's peace would have been perfect. Just one exception. Holding a razor blade in one hand and a nearly empty bottle of one-hundred-proof apple schnapps in the other, I brought the blade to my face. I was horrified at the image in the mirror. Here was a twenty-one-year-old woman, with long flowing curly blonde hair that fell to the middle of her back. Her blue eyes were bloodshot from crying for so long. Both of her arms had become raw from countless superficial cuts spanning the shoulder to her wrist, and across her chest and stomach.

To outsiders close and not-so-close, she was attractive, outgoing, and intelligent. She was a newly minted college graduate with a psychology degree. Everything seemed perfect to the intimate or casual observer. But the mirror told a different story. The girl in the mirror was fat and ugly, and I despised her completely. I wished more than anything for her to be dead. I fantasized about killing her. I had already poisoned her with rat poison. I even calculated how many boxes it would take, and I doubled that number. But she was too strong and survived. Why wouldn't she die?

With the razor blade at my temple, I stared ahead in the mirror as I cut straight away to my chin.

*Much better.*

Blood began to trickle down my face.

*Now what can I do?*

I lowered the razor to my chest making fresh cuts over the old ones from the previous week. I felt momentarily relieved that I had something tangible to show for what I felt inside.

The relief was fleeting. Guilt and confusion overwhelmed me in the next moment.

*Now look at what you did! You're so stupid. I HATE YOU! Die, you stupid fat pig.*

I slapped the image starring back at me and fell sobbing to the floor in the fetal position.

I lay on the floor motionless, waiting for my tears to subside. Jay Leno's funny, sharp monologue was on in the background, but I didn't bother to turn my head to watch. He never seemed to lack for material when it came to teasing or mocking celebrities. To him, everyone was the ideal target for a joke.

*I hate Jay Leno.*

I inhaled deeply as I gathered myself up and walked to my bed and sat down on the comforter. I picked up the phone and dialed a very familiar number.

"Hello."

The only word I could muster before sobbing took over.

"Lisa?"

"Yeah."

I was barely audible. The only language that seemed manageable was the sound of uncontrollable sobbing.

"Where are you?"

It was 10:37 on a mild spring Wednesday night.

"At home."

Alcohol always made me sound like a little girl—weak, powerless, scared, alone. It was the convenient escape of choice. But, the escape was hardly welcome. I felt lost in a cold, dark forest with no promise of rescue.

"What's the matter?"

She knew the answer already. She would sit patiently on the other end of the line, even if it would be minutes again before I spoke again.

"I hate myself. I wish I was dead. Besides, what's the point of living anyway?"

More silence followed. I always had a difficult time finding the right words to say.

*I don't know how I'm feeling. I feel a void. I feel empty. I feel alone.*

But I said none of these things to her.

"Where's your mom?"

"She's in bed sleeping."

I knew she was asking where she was to make sure I wasn't home alone so that if she needed to act immediately, she could call her for help.

"Have you been drinking?"

"Yes."

I was twisting the plastic phone cord around my finger.

"I'm never going to get better. I may as well die."

Again. A few moments of dead air.

"I just cut myself."

"Where?"

She was deliberate, calm in her questioning.

"It's no big deal."

I continued to twist the phone cord around my finger.

"Do you think that maybe you need go to mental health?"

She was careful not to sound urgent.

"No! I'm not a psycho, crazy person. Besides I can't go anyway because I've been drinking."

I knew the protocol: the policy of the county mental health was not to admit a person if he or she was under the influence of any drug, including alcohol. And, anyway, it was the only inpatient psychiatric unit in Redding.

"Well, why don't you go to bed right now and then when you wake up, come and see me? Can you make it to my office at ten tomorrow morning?"

"Uh huh."

My pain already was retreating, and the prospects of seeing Jaime eased my mind. I had grown to trust Jaime over the last seven months of working with her. She had a genuine tenderness that I so desperately needed. I soaked up her caring words and kindness like a thirst-starved sponge. No matter when, her voice always had that tender tone. Even in the middle of the night, she managed to avoid sounding croaky.

I woke up the next morning feeling much better than the previous night. I was going to see Jaime. She was small compared to my five-foot-nine-inch, medium-framed body—maybe a head shorter than me. Despite her size, she had aura of delicate strength—firm not fragile. Her dark, shoulder-length curly hair almost always was pulled back in two barrettes, one on either side of her face to show her clear, polished complexion. The most noticeable feature on her face was her smile—large, infectious.

It was early in April, so the crisp morning air rejuvenated me as I stepped out of my midnight blue 1995 Geo Storm. I walked down the concrete sidewalk that lined the busy street until I came to the red concrete steps at the front of Jaime's office. As I approached the windowless, dark oak door, I looked to my left at a brass plaque that had four gold names on it. The second showed Jaime's name.

I walked in as I had so many times in the past, but today was different. Jaime must have heard the door open because she was standing in the hallway outside her office as I walked in the front door. Our eyes met, suggesting this was no ordinary meeting. She looked at me with her large luminous brown eyes perched above a tired smile.

"Hi, Lisa. Come in."

The butterflies in my stomach had gradually intensified as I drew closer to her building and as I passed through the waiting room to her office. I passed Jaime in the doorway and settled where I always did—in a white wicker love seat tucked in the corner of her tiny office. She closed her door and followed behind me and sat in her white glider. It had a matching ottoman upon which she normally put her feet as we talked, but today she didn't put her feet up.

She made normal small talk for a few minutes, asking me how my morning had been and commented on how nice the weather was, but I remained on alert. Something felt out of our usual routine. My butterflies were fluttering even more rapidly.

"I have to tell you something," she said, leaning forward, putting her folded hands in her lap.

*I knew it.*

I was trying to prepare myself mentally for whatever was to come next. I didn't respond. Instead, I waited. Our conversations always had long spells of silence.

"You know that my parents live in the Bay Area and I go down there just about every weekend."

I nodded.

"It's a long drive, and it's really hard on my son."

She stopped for a second before continuing.

"I think it's really important for him to live close to his grandparents ... so I'm going to be moving down there to be closer to them."

The news hit as if I had been struck in the chest with a heavy object. I was paralyzed in time and space. My chest tightened with pressure. Everything shut down. The crisp bracing morning air was long forgotten.

*I knew this would happen,* I told myself. *She hates you. Everyone hates you. Everyone leaves you because you're worthless. I hate you. I wish you were dead.*

"Lisa."

Jaime spoke gently and softly.

"What?"

I was back in focus but still completely numbed by the news.

"We can still talk and have phone sessions. And you can come down to see me in the Bay Area sometimes for sessions, and I'm sure I'll be coming up here a lot. It's only a three-hour drive."

Her explanation sounded like a sales pitch well rehearsed for the intended benefit of any fill-in-the-blank client. The remainder of the session was a blur.

I left her office, walked the steps and down the street to my car. Not until I was buckled in the car would I allow myself to cry. For an hour, I cried until there were no tears left. Then, I started the car, put it in gear, and pulled away from the curb in my reliable Geo Storm. I drove around aimlessly for at least an hour before I made my decision.

*I'm going to go to the dam.*

I liked the peacefulness at the dam's location. Tall whispering pine trees swayed so perfectly in the gentle breeze: their perfectly natural conversation with me. When the lake was quiet, unpolluted with boaters, I could watch bald eagles dive deep into the lake to catch large salmon. I'm sure it would have made fishermen jealous to see the effortless nature of this great bird catching such a large fish in just mere seconds. I smiled at the thought. True to experience, the peaceful setting would be smothered with my dark thoughts that always bubbled to my troubled surface. The bucolic peace of my daydreams gradually but surely metamorphosed into the expected thoughts of suicide. This day, my dreams advanced further than they had before: I had dreamed of jumping off the dam.

Three weeks earlier, there was a story in the local newspaper, *The Record Searchlight,* about a twenty-one-year-old female who jumped to her death at this exact spot on the dam. I stood staring over the edge as a gust of wind blew my long blonde hair into my face. Sweeping it out of my face and behind my ears, I wondered what she must have been thinking as she fell hundreds of feet to her death on the concrete below.

So many people would go to the dam for a romantic evening, and I'd watch them; they always seemed so happy. And when I'd walk by them and smile, they'd always smile back. No one ever noticed what lurked behind my exterior appearance.

By the time I got to the dam, it was already late in the afternoon and the sun was going to set soon. But I didn't feel like walking across the dam because I didn't want anyone to see me. So I drove for a few more minutes until I found a secluded place with nearby walking trails.

*This is a perfect place. No one will bother me here.*

I parked my car in a small dirt pullout, and then sat for a few seconds feeling completely mellow. Sighing, I looked out the driver's side window only to see a small gray squirrel scurrying across the road with what looked like an acorn in his tiny mouth. I continued to watch him as he safely made it to the other side of the road. He dropped the acorn and began to study his prize. With my eyes still fixed on the little squirrel, I opened my car door, the sound scaring him, and he took off through the thick manzanita scrub brush until I could no longer see him.

Once out of my car, I put my cell phone, car keys, and an eight-ounce bottle of one-hundred-proof schnapps in the pocket of my green zip-up track jacket, a memento of my time on the college track team. With everything accounted for, I started up the short but very steep rocky trail in front of me.

It wasn't a trail designed for the public. It looked more like a trail that county workers used to reach the surrounding power lines. I walked down for a few minutes until I came to a substation where one could hear the loud buzzing from the enormous layer of energy surging above. A "Do Not Enter" sign was posted.

*Oh yeah, who's going to stop me.*

I put my hands around the first bar above my head. I had to make it to the first level of cross bars on the power line to reach the built-in ladder conveniently located for Pacific Gas and Electric workers.

I'm not exactly sure why I climbed the power line. It wasn't for the purpose of jumping off, but maybe it was the hope that I would slip and fall. I climbed until I could feel the ends of my hair on my body standing. The buzzing was so loud that it obscured any other noise. The surrounding air was stiflingly thick, so I decided to move down about ten feet.

Sitting more than one hundred feet above the rocky ground below, I looked out over the horizon and took in the exquisite beauty of the surrounding wilderness and far-off mountains. With the sun beaming in my eyes and the wind playing with my hair, I looked up into the rippling ocean of clouds and wondered where God was. If I fell from my perch, would I fall into his waiting arms or would I just find myself covered in a dusty grave only to live all of eternity in purgatory? The lake and dam looked eerily peaceful. In two months, the area would be occupied daily by laughing vacationers. I looked at my car from my perch. It seemed so small as did passing cars.

*I could stay here all night. No one would find me.*

The sun had started to set, and it was so beautiful. I took the alcohol I had carried up and took in a large mouthful, enough to create a burning sensation in the stomach. *After a few more swigs, I won't feel the burn anymore.*

The cell phone came alive.
"Hello."
"Where are you?"
It was Mom.
"Why do you want to know?"

I hated everyone at that moment, especially my mom. I couldn't understand why she wouldn't leave me alone. I could take care of myself. I was so sick and tired of everyone's prying stares, and I could feel the whispers behind my back.

*Ssshhh! Don't upset Lisa. She may go AWOL.*

Everyone—especially my mom—treated me like I was a breakable piece of a rare, treasured china set worth tens of thousands of dollars. I just wanted everyone to leave me alone. I didn't want to feel loved and cared for; I wanted to die.

"I'm just wondering. I was just starting to get worried."

I could hear the hurt in her voice. Pain from me shutting her out. The ache from watching her youngest daughter in such despair, unable to help. I didn't care.

In reality, I did care, toting the heavy burden of guilt every day for hurting my mom, which made the self-hate that much more intense. Her tears were ever present. I'd scream at her to leave me alone, and then I would hurt myself more because of the pain being inflicted upon someone who was completely genuine in her feelings and concerns.

I ended the call with my mom, drank the rest of the alcohol, and threw it as far as I could. I listened for the bottle crash, but it never came.

*Maybe it fell in some bushes.*

I decided to call Jaime.

I reached her answering service. The operators probably knew me by name by then because I called her almost every day after hours. The operator spoke up.

"Stay on the line while we get her, okay?"

"Okay."

I waited a few seconds, and she came back on line.

"We are patching you through."

"Lisa?"

Jaime was on the other end. Her calming voice was alone a significant bit of therapeutic comfort.

"Hi."

I sounded almost too chipper given my current predicament.

"What's going on?"

Jaime's protocol for crisis calls always seemed right.

"I'm stuck."

"What do you mean you're stuck?"

Her voice sounded as if she were puzzled, but perhaps this was deliberately so.

"Well, I climbed a power pole, and now it's too dark to see, and I can't get down."

"How did you get up there then?"

"It was light when I got here, so it was easy."

"Were you planning on jumping off?"

She asked calmly.

"NO! I just wanted to climb up here, but I didn't climb up to jump."

"Okay."

The hesitancy was probably deliberate. She was trying to quickly assess the situation and to see if indeed I was atop this precarious perch.

"Do you need me to help you?"

"I need a flashlight to get down. Can you bring me a flashlight?"

"Yes, where are you?"

"Are you going to call the police?"

I needed to know.

"Are you going to jump?" she countered.

"No."

"Okay, I promise I won't call the police. Now where are you?"

"I'm at the dam but just pulled off the side of the road. You'll see my car."

"Okay, it's been a long time since I've been up there, but I'm pretty sure I can remember."

"You don't know where the dam is?"

It was hard to believe that anyone around here didn't know where the dam was. Jaime quickly responded.

"I'll find it. But I first have to drop my son off somewhere, so it's going to take me a few minutes to get there, okay?"

"Don't forget the flashlight."

"I won't," and she hung up.

I sat on the power line in complete darkness. In the far distance to my right, I could see the city lights of the small city of

Redding, California. And to my left I could see the few lights that lined the entire four-hundred-foot length of the dam. I could feel and hear a gentle rustling breeze moving through the forest of pine trees around me. Fear and exhilaration mixed in an anxious moment of counterpoint.

About fifteen minutes had passed when I looked toward the road where my car was parked and saw a police car drive by at a low speed. My heart started to pump a little faster, but I knew she wouldn't have called the police because she promised. Another five minutes went by, and I watched as Jaime's maroon four-door Honda pulled into the dirt pullout and parked beside my little Geo Storm.

I watched as she and another woman I didn't recognize from so far away exit the car. I yelled out to her, but she couldn't hear me, but then I remembered my cell phone had a light on it so I opened my phone and waved it, thinking she would see the light, but she didn't. I watched as she and the mystery lady returned to the car and drove off.

*What the heck?!*

Then I saw a second police car slowly approach my car with his spotlight illuminating the dirt drive. They were looking for me. I didn't want to go to jail for climbing the power pole and would have rather died than go back to county mental health. The only reasonable option was to get down as fast as possible.

In the darkness, I felt around for the ladder.

*There it is.*

Once I had my hands where they needed to be, I had to lift my legs over a group of bars and then squeeze through a narrow hole to reach the ladder. As I was squeezing through the hole, my foot slipped, and I started to fall, but my arm was hooked by a bar.

However, the rest was easy, an uneventful climb down the ladder to the bottom rung still five feet off the ground. During daylight, it would have been no big deal because the ground could be easily seen, but in complete darkness, it was quite a bit more difficult. Climbing up, I had to reach up over my head and jump to get to the first cross bar. Hanging down, it wouldn't be too far of a drop, but there was no time to waste, so it was a matter of just letting go and dropping. When my feet hit the rocky uneven ground I fell to my knees.

*That probably would've hurt if I was sober.*

Once on my feet, I started running to my car. Knowing the second police car had just passed, I figured that reaching my car quickly enough would allow me to probably beat him out to the main road and then lose him.

At the car, there was still no sign of the police. With heart racing from the adrenaline and hands shaking, I managed to put the keys in the ignition and spun out of the small dirt drive onto the paved road.

I made it.

The relief was premature. Pulling through the intersection, I saw three police cruisers waiting, and I saw the fourth through my rearview mirror, his bubble-gum top activated, motioning me to pull over.

*Shit!*

Now stopped, I rolled down my window, knowing all too well that the alcohol breath would be easily noticed. An olive-skinned, black-haired male officer in his mid- thirties walked up to the car and leaned down so that I could see his dark brown eyes.

"Are you Lisa Leachman?"

"Yeah. What's wrong?"

I answered, grinning a bit mischievously because I knew the answer to my own question.

"Could you step out of the car, please?"

I left my car and was amazed when I saw five police cars with two officers per car surrounding me. The scene resembled one of a suspected felon—a bank robber, perhaps—being circled. I just looked blankly at the closest officer because he was obviously the one taking charge. He was an average-looking man who stood a head taller than me. He seemed nice enough. He was gentle in his speaking tone and wasn't at all bossy or pushy like many officers could be at a scene like this.

"So," he began in a gentle tone, "we got a call from your counselor. She told us you climbed a power pole. Were you going to hurt yourself?"

"No."

I looked to the officer standing beside the man in charge. I smiled, deciding to be matter of fact in tone.

"Haven't you ever wanted to climb up one?"

I paused, still smiling.

"I've always wanted to."

"Actually, yeah, I have."

He returned a smile, a sign that I could confidently talk myself out of this self-inflicted mess.

"It was really cool."

"Well, your counselor did tell us that you told her that you weren't up there to kill yourself."

"I wasn't."

At that moment, Jaime approached, with the strange lady in tow. Up close, I recognized her with her short light-colored hair framing her fifty-something face; she worked in the same building as Jaime. She was the default backup—the co-therapist—in case a personal crisis arose whenever Jaime was out of town. She had an air of superiority about her as if she were wiser and more experienced than Jaime. I didn't like her for that reason; I thought she was too arrogant and insincere.

Jaime stepped forward and introduced herself to the officers. She began by telling them the need for her client to be taken to the mental health facility. Utter betrayal took over. First, she told me she was moving away, then called the police on me, and now she's trying to talk them into having her trusting client locked up in the loony bin.

My coyish tone now morphed into childlike desperation.

"Please don't take me to mental health. I'm fine. I was a little upset earlier. That's why I called her, but I'm fine now."

Jaime was just as passionate to get me admitted as I was to stay out of the hospital.

"You know," Jaime began, staring the olive-skinned officer in his dark eyes, "she really should go to mental health."

"No!"

I began by pleading with her but soon realized the officer was the one I had to convince, so I turned my full attention to him.

"I promise I didn't climb that pole to hurt myself."

I repeated this as I stared into his exhausted eyes. He looked as if he were at the end of his shift and wanted this escapade to end as quickly as possible.

Jaime and I continued to argue our cases for about ten minutes until I eventually won the debate with the officer. He told her to go to her car because she was upsetting me. Jaime looked at me and then back to the officer.

Clearly neither of us was going to cede this debate easily. The strange lady stepped forward out of the shadows to stand next to Jaime, possibly to support her. I didn't like her being there, and I really didn't like her putting her nose in my business. She stood by Jaime telling her that they should leave and to let the police take over. But Jaime didn't listen to her. Like me, she stood her ground.

Death would have been the preferred alternative to being returned to that facility. Jaime walked back to her car, obviously upset and irritated by the turn of events, and then she turned around one last time.

"You really should take her to mental health. That's where she needs to be right now."

I was so mad at her, knowing as long as she was there, my chances of being admitted to mental health were growing. The options were narrowing rapidly.

"Just leave," I screamed.

She just looked at me, shook her head, and walked away with the co-therapist.

Again, here came the ache of guilt and remorse for yelling at her, but no other choice seemed apparent.

*Why did she do that to me?*

Once Jaime left the scene, the rest was easy. The battle had been won or at least I thought. Dismissive of everything Jaime had just told the officers, I added that she was a moron and didn't know what she was talking about and that I was perfectly capable of taking care of myself and there was no way at all that I was suicidal. They were more than willing to accept that as an answer because exhaustion was taking its toll on the olive-skinned officer.

"Do you promise to go straight home?" the officer in charge asked.

"Yes, I promise. I'll go home!"

Not wanting to risk any about-face, I did just that.

It was nearing ten thirty when I pulled into the safety of my dirt driveway and parked my car behind my mom's old four-door red Bronco. The lingering odor of our freshly painted yellow house filled my nose as I stepped out of my car. I didn't like the boldness of the yellow color when it was being painted, but it also had grown on me and now I actually was quite fond of it. Thankfully, my mom had left the porch light on for me, so I climbed the four concrete steps effortlessly before reaching the front door.

The only light on in the house was a small Tiffany lamp on a little redwood table next to the brown suede couch in the living room. I walked through the living room, guided by the small amount of light, feeling extremely guilty for treating Jaime so badly. Once in my bedroom, I dialed her number. She spoke as soon as she answered, knowing it was me.

"Hi, Lisa. Are you home?"

Her tone was different. Not raised—in fact, almost like her usual steady cadence—but it was tinged with anger, disappointment, weariness.

"Yes."

"Are you okay?"

"Yeah, I just didn't want to go to mental health. I hate it there," I spoke softly.

"I know you do."

She paused for a brief second.

"We need to talk. Come to my office in the morning at nine? Can you do that?"

Jaime's question was a command.

"Yeah."

"Then I'll see you tomorrow at nine."

I had to wake up early to make the twenty-five-minute drive to Jaime's office in order to be there by nine that morning. I felt nervous walking up to the entryway of her office, not having any idea of what either of us would say to each other after last night's dramatic, awkward encounter.

When I opened the front door to the office, I immediately saw Jaime standing alone in the small waiting room. At her right, a small blue couch was adorned with two floral throw pillows. In front of the blue couch, a small oak coffee table was covered in magazines. She smiled as I walked in, and she then motioned for me to follow her into her office. Sitting in the usual chair, I knew that this was no routine encounter. Her stiff body language suggested that this wasn't going to be pleasant or easy.

"I was up all night thinking about what happened last night, and I just can't do that anymore."

She paused as if she wanted to canvass my immediate reaction.

"I have a five-year-old son, and I just can't be up all night—all of the time—worrying about you all of the time."

No words came out of my mouth. I just sat listening, waiting for the inevitable.

"It's just too risky and dangerous for me to try to work with you when I'm living three hours away."

My chest and throat burned as I struggled to hold back the tears, using every bit of control not to blink because I knew the tears would be unleashed in uncontrolled torrents. An excruciatingly long silence followed. Several minutes passed before Jaime spoke again.

"I just I can't work with you anymore."

I looked down at my feet in silence to escape her stare.

"You need to work with someone close to you. I know some really good people that you'd like."

I just shook my head no because if I spoke only sobs would have come.

"I want you to drive with me to Guardian Hospital and admit to their outpatient program."

Again I shook my head no. And, again, several more minutes of silence passed.

"I'll go with you, but we would have to leave soon."

Once again, my defiant nod of the head. I wouldn't look at her. I couldn't. Otherwise sobs would have overtaken the room.

I had never cried before anyone—except in the manageable distance on a phone line—and the current situation wasn't going to change my habit. Although, it seemed that some sense of relief would have occurred had I unleashed the barrel of tears that seemed to press against every square inch inside my body.

Jaime switched gears, and tried a different tactic: pleading.

"Please, will you go?"

"No."

I rolled my eyes.

"Please."

She seemed to stretch out the single syllable for maximum effect.

I stared at her for a few seconds, feeling irritated that she was saying "please," and knowing that I hated saying no to her when she was saying "please."

"Sorry. It's too expensive. I can't."

My words suddenly sounded therapeutic.

"Well, I called your mom, and she said she could come up with enough money."

In silence, I felt my will to resistance escape. Jaime called and talked to my mother occasionally, knowing clearly that I would be anything but supportive.

Again, silence. Racking my brain, I was fighting futilely to find a good reason not to go. Thirty minutes passed in an uncomfortable, agonizing silence. It felt like it would never end. She'd ask me to go, and then I'd answer shaking my head no. Then more silence. Then she'd ask me again to go, and I'd give the same response. Our normal one-hour session was coming to an end.

I figured at some point she'd give up, but she didn't. And eventually, after what seemed an eternity, she played her last card with deep sincerity.

"Please, Lisa, will you do it for me?"

This time no head shaking. I looked up at her, and that was all. It was the green light she was waiting for, and there was no time to let another spell of silence reverse the course of what she had fought for with unrelenting discipline.

My internal fog cleared enough for the drive to the outpatient psychiatric facility, my home for the next six weeks of my life.

I had won a small battle the night before with the police officers, but Jaime had won the war, making the case for Guardian Hospital.

# Chapter 2

## Meeting Mark

*Six months later*

I was never planning on going to another therapist again after Jaime moved away. My heart ached from missing her, and I would never allow myself to be hurt again. But when I started my master's degree program in May of 2000, one requirement for graduation was to have sixty hours of personal psychotherapy.

I hated the prospect of enduring another round of therapy, telling the story again, working slowly to cultivate trust with someone. Hardly ready to face the challenge, I also realized that in order to graduate, I would have to find a new therapist.

Yet, a new round of therapy was desperately needed.

At first, I went to a local nonprofit counseling center, a full stable of inexperienced therapist interns. This was the perfect place for me to skate by to meet the sixty-hour therapy requirement.

Not getting the option to select a therapist, I was assigned to whoever was available, which was fine. My therapist was a middle-aged woman, likely in her forties. One session was all I needed to deem her completely worthless. The most irritating thing was her insistent return to Jaime and her stubborn attempts to see her trying to align herself with me by bringing Jaime down. I quickly began to feel extremely defensive.

"Stop talking about her like you know her," I told her angrily with a finality that this ruse was going to end.

"You don't know her, and you don't know me."

I glared, daring her to speak, but she just sat there in silence.

"How could you possibly know what was going on in her life?"

Knowing that there would be no second session with this intern, I started asking her questions deliberately difficult for her to answer. Meaningless words stumbled clumsily out of her mouth.

*Poor lady, she has absolutely no clue what's going on.*

I felt sorry for her in some small way, as she sat fidgeting in her chair, trying haphazardly to search for the next thing to say. But that didn't stop me from running her through the gauntlet. For the rest of the hour, I was cruel. It felt satisfying, but I quickly got bored. Finally, the one-hour session was over, and I could tell she was just as glad to get me out of the office.

Back to the drawing board in finding a therapist. I knew Jaime's dad was still traveling to Redding seeing clients, but I didn't think that I would feel comfortable talking to him. Mainly, I didn't want to work with a man, so for the time being, he was out of the question.

Three weeks passed and I still hadn't found a therapist, but then again I wasn't looking. Time was running short. I was the only one in my class who hadn't found a therapist, so I knew that procrastinating was no longer possible. One evening during a ten-minute break in a class, I overheard a couple of my classmates talking about the name Mark Smith, which immediately piqued my interest.

"Who are you guys talking about?" I asked.

"We are both seeing the same therapist," my two fellow classmates said almost in tandem.

"Who is it?"

"Mark Smith."

"Do you like him?"

"Yeah, we both really like him. We were just talking about how smart he is and that a lot of times what he says goes over our heads."

They both started laughing.

The instructor walked back in the room, so we had to stop talking but Smith was intriguing. I wanted to talk to him merely for the fact that he was Jaime's beloved mentor, but also now a challenge had settled in my mind: to either prove he wasn't so smart or to prove that they were really dumb.

One thing was for sure: I wasn't planning on really getting any kind of psychological help of any kind from him. It would be an academic exercise with the right distance, just enough to complete the graduate school requirement.

The next morning I made the phone call.

"Hello."

A male voice answered the phone.

"Hi, I'm a student at National University, and I have to have sixty hours of

therapy."

I was nervous just being on the phone with him, as if he already knew my history. "I was wondering if I could make an appointment to see you."

I got the words out as fast as I could. A part of me hoped that he wouldn't be available to take on any new clients.

"Oh, okay, let me get my appointment book. Hold on a second."

I waited, wondering if this was as good an idea as it seemed when it emerged during my night class.

"Okay, how about this Wednesday at either 10:00 a.m. or 4:00 p.m.?"

"How about 4:00 p.m.?"

Uncertainty took over.

"Okay, then I'll see you Wednesday."

He ended the conversation.

I was nervous when I drove up to his office, facing this with a closed mind and full body armor.

*I'm not going to let him penetrate my mind, and I sure the heck am not going to develop any kind of meaningful relationship with him.*

The office was a surprise. It had the size and appearance of a humble shack, rundown and old, a relic stubbornly clinging to a sophisticated contemporary landscape. Sitting in my blue Geo Storm mustering up enough courage to go inside, I continued to study the small building. A large stained-glass still life of a butterfly was in the window.

*That's kind of pretty.*

A loud mob of voices broke my thoughts. Looking over to my right, I saw what looked like thirty-plus teenagers crossing the street, playfully teasing each other, just in their own world, seemingly having a good time. I looked to my black-and-pink Timex running watch that read 4:00 p.m.

*School must have just gotten out.*

Suddenly I realized that I had procrastinated too long and needed to approach the unknown territory of this new therapist.

The only thing standing in my way were a few twisted old oak trees and cracked cement through which some weeds had pushed their way in order to find the life of the sun. I breathed deeply, considering what I would say to him. I exited my car and walked across the cracked cement driveway to the light brown painted door and softly knocked.

*Maybe he won't hear me and won't answer the door.*

No such luck. He opened the door, and standing before me was not at all what I expected: the salt-and-pepper hair; the clear, smooth face; a slim fit man of between fifty and sixty at most. His hair was pulled back into a ponytail, which is what threw me more than anything else.

"Hi, I'm Mark. Come in," he said in a kind gentle voice.

His large brown eyes were warm sparkling gems of life.

"Hi," I answered in almost a whisper.

*This is going to be easy. He's not scary at all.*

We stood eye to eye, and he put out his right hand for me. His hand fortified his confident, strong bearing. His strength, gentle and visceral at once, was instantaneously calming.

"Please sit down."

"Where?"

I had three options; I could choose his chair obviously his because it was beside his messy desk or an ugly, old, green, worn out chair that was accompanied by an equally ugly, old, green, worn out ottoman, or a fairly sterile uncomfortable-looking wooden rocking chair.

"Anywhere you want."

What I really wanted to do was to sit in his chair. I've always wanted to sit in the therapist's chair, just to see what would happen. I imagined all sorts of scenarios—hostile, awkward, whimsical, authoritarian, etc. However, I resisted the urge and chose the rocking chair mainly because the rocker was right next to the door (in case a surprise exit was necessary). Also, the ugly green ensemble had to be avoided by all means.

"So tell me about yourself."

Mark settled into his uncomfortable-looking wooden chair and propped his arm up on his matching light-colored walnut desk that resembled a kitchen table converted amateurishly into a desk.

I was too busy taking in the surroundings to answer right away. The large wooden bookshelf almost took up half of the tiny room. It was exceptionally messy—books and papers were everywhere in piles on the green carpeted floor and his desk. The only natural light in the room came from the one window in the office, which was where his desk was sitting. Several piles of papers lay disorganized on his desk.

*Should I tell him that his office is really messy?*

"Your office is full of a lot of stuff."

This would be a little nicer than telling him it was a mess.

"Yeah, I have a lot of stuff in here."

"A lot of books. Have you read them all?"

I hoped this stalling tactic would give me the necessary time to come up with the "politically correct" answers.

"I've read through all of them. Some I've only bought to read certain chapters."

"How can you find anything on your desk?"

"I know where everything is."

"Can you tell me something about yourself?"

Only now was there was a slight crack in his pleasant demeanor, a glint of irritation really only perceptible to a prospective patient who had no genuine desire for constructive therapy. Now that I felt like I had a tiny bit of power, I felt a little more comfortable telling him something about me.

I looked at him.

"Yes, I can. What do you want me to say?"

"Whatever you want."

He leaned back in his chair and waited, acting as if the daily march of time had been suspended at his convenience.

Now I was more than a bit perplexed.

*How am I supposed to answer that? Is it a trick question? What does he really want to know?*

All that really mattered was Jaime. I missed her so very much, my heart ached, but I couldn't tell him about that. At least not yet. The only logical place was to talk about the beginning of my descent.

# Chapter 3

# Eating Poison

It was June 1999 when I determined what, I thought, was a suicide plan. I found the perfect poison: D-Con, the popular rat poison brand, and all I had to do was drive to the grocery store to get it. I knew that I would have to consume a lot of boxes in order for it to work, but at least I knew it would fulfill the objective. I figured one box could kill three or four rats, and I guessed the average rat weighed maybe two or three pounds, so fifteen boxes would be more than enough.

I felt relieved deciding to eat the poison because finally I would be able to break free of the horrible pain that had been paralyzing me for the last few months.

My initial plan was to run and exercise five to six hours daily in the extreme heat, while starving myself of food and water. It wasn't unusual for the August temperature in Redding to hit 110 degrees. I hoped to drop dead from dehydration while out running on the trails. But that plan wasn't working, and depression's burden increased with each day.

The intended date for my plan seemed suddenly almost exhilarating among the endless march of ordinary hot summer days in Redding. The thought of death was a little scary, but I figured that was only because of my Catholic upbringing and the early childhood sermons that our priest would give on Sunday mornings, frequently about purgatory, the horrible dark place sinners go to live out all of eternity. But I didn't care about the church, and I didn't care about God. He forgot about me a long time ago, so therefore I could forget about him. I wasn't so sure that I believed in purgatory anyway. So I felt more excitement than anything else.

*I'll finally be free of this world. No more pain, no more darkness.*

I drove to a local Safeway and purchased a brown bag filled with packages of D-Con before going across the street to a McDonald's for a chocolate milkshake. Now, it was a matter of finding the ideal location to consume all of this. I ended up at a local Little League ballpark, the only place with no people in the middle of a scorching afternoon. Normally the ballpark would be filled, but an afternoon temperature reading of 111 degrees had taken its toll on outdoor activities.

I left my Geo Strom with my chocolate milkshake in one hand and the brown paper sack in the other and went inside the green dugout. Sitting on the hot, green wooden bench, I stared out at the baseball field, reminiscing over the many games I had played out on this same field over the years…

\*\*\*\*

Come on, Leese.
"Hit a home run!" my mom yelled from the green bleachers. I looked over at her and everyone else in the crowd and playfully stuck my tongue out at them.

I stepped up to the diamond plate and got into my stance to show the pitcher that I was ready. My coach's voice rang in my ears.

"Never swing on the first pitch. Wait for the first strike."

I always hated that rule, but nevertheless I waited. The first ball came hurtling through the air, and I just stood watching as it flew past me.

"Strike one," the umpire yelled.

*Okay, now I'm ready,* I thought as I returned to my stance. As soon as the second the ball left the pitcher's hand, I knew it would be a perfect hit. My eye never left the ball, and as it came into my hitting zone, I swung the bat with all my might. "Crack."

The ball flew through the air, and I waited just a split second before taking off to round the bases. I knew I would make it a home run even though the ball fell short of cresting the fence. My all-time favorite thing to do was to psych out the other team. I made it to second base before the ball made it back into the infield, but I wasn't finished because I would make it to home base.

I stepped off second base to taunt the girl playing shortstop who had the ball in hand. I stared into her eyes—not budging—just waiting for her to throw the ball to tag me out.

I took two more steps toward third base, and predictably, she threw the ball to the girl standing next to me. I took off toward third base and, like clockwork, the girl who had freshly caught the ball threw it to the third baseman, but by then I was already halfway to the home plate.

The crowds were on their feet cheering and yelling—half telling me to stop and the other half cheering me onto home. With absolutely no fear, I charged the catcher who was waiting for the ball. By the determined look on her face, I knew the ball was soon to grace her mitt, so I slid to the ground, finding my foot on the home plate before she could tag me out.

A slushy drip from my chocolate milkshake brought me back to the present.

*What the heck?*

I looked down at my bare leg as the droplets of milkshake found their way down my right leg and rested on my shoe. I looked around for a napkin but couldn't find one.

*Oh well.*

Then with a slight shade of trepidation, I tipped the box of rat poison back toward my mouth almost as if I was ready to down a shot of Jose Cuervo. Only this time, the poison would be followed by a milkshake chaser. Almost instantly, I could feel my stomach begin to revolt against the poisonous contents, so I closed my eyes to concentrate.

*It's not that bad, it's not that bad, it's not that bad. It's just a milkshake.*

I only made it through five of the boxes before a car drove by. The prospect of being discovered alarmed me, so I shoved the poison back into the grocery bag and threw the sack in the trash can. Only after hurrying back to the car and driving away from the park did the thought of the expense come to mind.

*I'm not going to waste it.*

I drove back to the trashcan in the park and grabbed the paper sack.

*I'm going to have to finish this somewhere else.*

I decided home would be the best place to finish what was started in the hot, dusty dugout. I pulled into my dirt circular driveway, determined to finish the job. I had to consume the rest of the boxes of poison before my mom and stepdad came home from work, which could be at any moment because they both owned their own businesses and often came home at different times of the day for whatever reason. I went directly to my bedroom and shut the door, feeling giddy and even more exhilarated than what I had been in the park. I finished off the remaining ten boxes with no problem.

*Now all I have to do is wait.*

I lay in my bed and closed my eyes.

I opened my eyes the next morning to find that I was still alive. I turned to look at the clock sitting on my nightstand—8:45 a.m. I was so angry because I had another day to get through—another day wishing and praying that this one would be my last.

*Maybe it just takes some time to work.*

My spirits began to quickly rise.

A couple of days passed without incident. I was waiting for even the smallest sign that my body was shutting down, but physically I continued to feel great. I began to think God was playing tricks on me. I knew I had eaten enough poison, but nothing was happening. I was furious.

*Why won't you let me die? I'll show you.*

I drove back to the grocery store. With my purchase in hand, I drove to the same dugout that I had visited a few days before and, just like last time, I sat on the same green wooden bench. With great determination, unlike the first time, I consumed the six new boxes I had just bought. This time, without even the slightest tint of trepidation. Now I was a pro—the taste wasn't bad at all. It just tasted like I was eating grass or hay; it was the texture that gagged me. All the little turquoise pellets filled my mouth, and I could feel every single one fighting its way down my esophagus.

*This time something has to happen.*
　I buried the evidence deep in an old metal trash can. But again, several days passed, and there still was no sign of any ill effects. I was confused and irritated; I knew for sure God was playing tricks on me.
*I guess I'll just have to think of something else.*
　I knew we had several guns: two hunting rifles and a shotgun, and a few old-fashioned black powder muzzleloaders that were my stepdad's favorites. However, not one was kept in the main house. Ever since we had been burglarized a couple years before, my stepdad kept the guns in a gun safe stored in a shed secured with an intrusion alarm. Knowing the shed was out of the question, I remembered that my biological dad always kept a handgun on his nightstand.
　A week passed since I had consumed the first wave of boxes of poison, when something finally happened. It was a late afternoon on a Friday when I was brushing my teeth. Apparently, the bristles of the toothbrush hit my gum line and blood quickly filled my mouth. I looked in the mirror and saw that all of my teeth were covered in blood, and it began to spill out of my mouth. I was ecstatic: finally something was happening. I didn't know what it was, but I knew it wasn't good.
　I figured the bleeding wouldn't last, and that it would soon stop, but it didn't. Over the next hour, I was cheerful, almost giddy as a steady stream of bright oxygen-rich blood continued to overspill my mouth.
　My mom came home immediately from work after my stepdad called her to tell her what was happening. As she pulled her tan 1989 Honda Accord into the driveway, dust flew into the air, making it temporarily unhealthy. I saw that she had a concerned look on her face when she saw me standing outside on the sidewalk with blood splattered everywhere. She exited her car, confused and startled at the sight of blood. As she approached me, she looked down at the sidewalk, its asphalt covered with blood from the endless stream of spit that spewed out of my poisoned mouth. Within every five seconds or so, my mouth would be so full of blood that I'd spit. Otherwise, I would have choked.

"What happened?"

She tried heroically to mask her worry.

I shrugged my shoulders. Any attempt to speak would have meant a wide-ranging splatter of blood.

"I'll be right back. I'm calling the hospital."

She scrambled up the stairs and was out of sight, dialing for the twenty-four-hour nurse line. I stayed outside, personally pleased about what I had done. She came back out perhaps just ninety seconds or so later, now with her purse on her shoulder.

"Come on. We're going to the hospital."

# Chapter 4

## The Hospital

As soon as we passed through the doors at the emergency department, my mom walked directly to the service desk to check me into the hospital. I was standing behind her, taking in the surroundings. *The last time I was here,* I thought to myself, *was when I was in the fifth grade.* My brother was in the eighth grade, and had shot himself. I still could remember clearly the numbness I felt when I heard the news.

The look of horror on my mom's face while she was on the phone receiving the news was forever burned into my memory. She dropped the phone and fell to her knees, sobbing with her face cradled into her hands. My stepdad grabbed the phone to find out what happened. Both my sister and I were crying before we even knew what happened.

It took a few minutes before we received the details. My stepdad filled us in with all the information after he got off the phone.

"He's okay. The bullet just went through his hand and leg. He's fine, just a little scared. He's on his way to the hospital, so we need to go."

"He's okay?" my mom asked, wiping the tears from her eyes.

"Yes."

My stepdad embraced my mom, who was now regaining control of her emotions.

"Well," my mom said in between sobs, "all Danny said to me was that Troy shot himself and was in an ambulance on the way to the hospital."

She started crying again.

"What a horrible way to tell someone that their child had been injured. I thought he was dead."

She let out a gut-wrenching moan as she fell limp into my stepdad's arms.

The entire way to the hospital no one said a word. I sat in the back seat staring out the rain-soaked window, silently crying, watching a passing parade of now-forgotten buildings and cars.

* * * * *

The middle-aged woman at the receptionist's desk reminded me of Rose from the hit eighties television show *The Golden Girls*, with her short red hair and snooty attitude.

"What's the problem?" She asked my mom as she looked us both over, trying to discover why on earth we were there.

"My daughter's mouth is bleeding."

The lady rolled her eyes a bit and looked almost annoyed that we were there wasting her time.

"What happened?"

She glared directly at me. I couldn't answer because my mouth was full of blood and it would have splattered everywhere. I just held out my hands—a gesture of helplessness.

"She can't talk because of the blood," my mom explained.

"Well she's going to have to."

The woman's tone was cold, bureaucratic.

I slightly opened my mouth attempting to speak when blood trickled out of my mouth onto her counter and paperwork.

"Sorry," I gurgled.

"OH! That's a lot of blood. Come back here into my area, so you can spit in my garbage can."

At the trash can, I spit a full mouth of blood. She watched with an odd fascination.

"Wow!"

Her attitude immediately changed as she became extremely sympathetic and helpful.

Once she saw how badly my mouth was bleeding, everything began to move very quickly. I was put into a hospital gown and in an ER bed. My arm was being poked with needles as the nurse filled ten vials of blood.

"Why are there so many vials?"

I was worried that they would figure out my secret. Although, on one hand, I wanted them to figure it out because I so desperately wanted help. But, on the other hand, I wanted to give up. I was tired of fighting this life.

"We need to find out what is wrong with you."

Her tone had now switched completely to genuinely felt compassion.

"If you keep taking all my blood, I'm going to run out pretty soon."

"It looks like a lot, but it isn't."

She continued to fill the vials.

I was happy, smiling and joking with all of the hospital staff. Happy to finally feel that I had succeeded. However, just then I noticed a tall, thin, man walk past my bed. His black hair was beginning to thin, revealing a receding hairline. His black pants and maroon long-sleeved button-up shirt matched his dark complexion well. I made eye contact with him and smiled as he passed.

I heard him ask the person in the next bed, "Are you Lisa Leachman?" Then I saw him again, but this time he looked a little confused.

"Are you Lisa?"

I just nodded my head and smiled.

"Hi, I'm Dr. Freeman, the hematologist."

He walked up to my bed with his hand stretched for me to shake it.

"Hi."

I was feeling cheerful, wondering if he already knew what I had really done. He asked my mom to leave and then he did all of the normal doctor routine things: listening to my heart and lungs and asking the usual medical history questions.

How old are you? Have you ever been hospitalized before? Are you currently taking any drugs whether legally or illegally?

My answer to all of his questions was a shake of my head signaling no. My medical history was unscarred and perfect in every way. And, then he looked straight to my blue eyes.

"Is there anything you want to tell me before I bring your mom back in?"

I looked directly into his slightly almond-shaped dark eyes and shook my head no. He knew, and I was just waiting for the cards to drop. He opened the thin curtain and motioned for my mom to come back into the room. Dread filled me as I waited for him to tell her that I had been eating poison.

"The test results came back from the blood smear, and it looks like it could possibly be leukemia."

He looked first at my mom and then at me. I was shocked that he didn't tell her I had poison coursing though my veins.

"I think someone may have messed up on the test, and I'm going to have them do it again just to be sure."

"Leukemia? So what's next?" my mom asked.

"I'm going to have her admitted to the hospital until we can get the bleeding under control, and I'm going to have some more tests run."

Then he put his hand on my shoulder.

"I'll be back in the morning to check in on you and hopefully your mouth will have stopped bleeding."

I smiled.

"Thanks."

And, with that single word, he left the room.

I glared at the male nurse who was torturing me as he tried to insert the IV. Three times he stuck the needle in my arm, and three times he missed my vein.

"This never happens to me. I never miss."

"Well you've missed three times on me."

The last few minutes had been a whirlwind tour of emotions. Everything was now moving so quickly after so many weeks of waiting. There would be no turning back now; I had no other choice but to ride this wave until the end. I was starting to wish I was back home because I hated the constant attention and prying eyes.

Now I was being plainly sarcastic to the incompetent man sticking me with huge IV needles.

"Well, you have really thick skin. I've never seen this before. I'm going to go get someone else to do it, okay?"

I just nodded my head.

A female nurse in her late thirties came over and got it in the first try. I smiled at her in appreciation, and she winked in return and then left. Once the IV was finally inserted and secured, I was finally leaving the ER. After five hours of sitting in the ER, I was finally being taken down the hall to the oncology unit.

"Why am I going to oncology? Isn't that for people with cancer?"

The nurse who had inserted the IV successfully was pushing my wheelchair.

"Yeah, but your doctor is an oncologist and hematologist, so you have to be where he does his rounds."

As we entered the oncology ward, the nurse opened the door and didn't completely latch it to keep it open and the door slammed into the right side of the wheelchair. A male nurse happened to see the "accident," and he looked at me with wide eyes, probably waiting to see my reaction. I turned to the nurse pushing me.

"How long have you been driving this thing?"

I started laughing. She apologized, embarrassed at what happened. The male nurse laughed along with me and teased her for letting the door hit a wheelchair-bound patient.

It was 4:30 a.m., only a half an hour before the sun was going to rise the next morning, when I was awakened by the same male nurse I had met the night before. He took my blood pressure, which read normal 120/60. For me, it always read 120/60. After a night of being on Vitamin K, blood was still in my mouth, but now it was gooey and sticky. I got out of bed and tried to get to the sink to rinse my mouth out, but I couldn't because one arm was connected to the IV and the other was being held hostage by the tightly binding blood pressure instrument.

Later that morning, Dr. Freeman, the hematologist, came by. Wearing a Hawaiian-print long-sleeve button-up shirt with khaki slacks, he came walking into my solo room with a bright smile on his face. Without hesitation, he walked over to the thick brown curtains and opened them, letting the eager sun finally awaken my darkened room. He reminded me of a friendly Jewish person with his big nose and dark skin.

"That's better," he said to me with a smile.

I had been studying for my abnormal psychology final that was going to take place that Monday night, which only gave me a couple of days to study. I took my eyes off my textbook when Dr. Freeman spoke.

"How are you doing?"

"I'm fine."

"Your mouth has stopped bleeding. That's good."

"Uh huh."

"What is that you're reading?"

He noticed my textbook.

"I'm studying for a psychology test."

"Psychology, huh? Is that your major?

"Yeah, I'm graduating this December with my bachelor's degree."

He sat at the edge of the hospital bed.

"You know, I found that a lot of the people who go into psychology do so to try to fix themselves."

His eyes were fixed squarely on mine.

"Did you know that?"

"I think I've heard something about that."

I returned to my reading. The room was quiet for a few moments.

"Well is there anything that you'd like to talk about before I leave?"

"No."

I knew he wanted me to confess about eating the rat poison, but I couldn't. I wasn't ready to talk. I desperately wanted help, but even though I felt like he truly cared and was so very kind and compassionate, I still couldn't break down the all-consuming solid steellike wall that had grown around me. I was paralyzed, afraid of what would happen, and I didn't want anyone to know what I had done. The embarrassment was overwhelming.

The next two days blurred together with the hourly blood draws, regular changes of IV bags, and blood pressure checks. Family and friends came and went. My mom was the most frequent visitor, coming several times every day, occasionally with my stepdad in tow.

One evening around six-thirty, my mom and stepdad came walking into my room, and when I looked up at her, I saw that her eyes were bloodshot from crying. I didn't ask what was wrong because I knew it was my fault, and that made my heart burn with pain. Two minutes later my biological dad and stepmom came by, and they all greeted each other as if they had met each other for the first time. Little did they know that I overheard the four of them fighting out in the hall moments earlier.

"Don't you know what's going on, Steve?" my mom sternly said to my dad, trying to keep her voice down so that no one could hear, but I could hear.

"What are you talking about?"

He was irritated by the confrontation.

"You're youngest daughter is in there because she tried to kill herself. Do you understand what that means?"

"It's not my fucking fault. Why are you yelling at me?"

"Well maybe because you're acting as if this is no big deal!" she yelled, forgetting that she was supposed to be talking quietly.

"I think she just wants attention."

"Well, her doctor asked me yesterday if she had ever been molested."

My dad stood silently as my mom continued.

"Do you think your dad could have messed with her, too?"

All hell broke loose.

"My dad is the greatest man I have ever known, and he would never touch one of his grandchildren in a sexual way."

"Well, why did he go to jail for molesting your brother's kids then, Steve?" she responded with a shaky voice. I knew she was fighting back tears.

"Those girls were screwed up in the head and were being feed all sorts of shit. He never molested them, and he never molested Lisa."

Lying in my bed, I turned my back in disgust, trying to block out the noise of the all-consuming fight. Suddenly, I remembered a recurring dream that always had a faceless man.

I was standing in an old wooden toolshed, crammed with every tool one could possibly imagine. Standing right in front of me was a man, but all I could see of him was his old dirty work jeans that hung loosely on his body and a pair of lace-up brown leather work boots. He didn't touch me, but would begin unzipping his pants, and I knew what I was supposed to do even though I didn't see it in my dream. I could smell the hay from the hay barn that was only ten feet away. It was musty and hot. Anytime I had this dream, I would wake up, my pillow drenched in my sweat.

"Hi, sweetheart."

My dad came up to my bedside and gave me a kiss, followed closely by his wife Vicky.

My mom stayed quiet and only made meaningless small talk with my dad. That was the only time my dad came up to see me.

My maternal grandma came once or twice. I referred to her as Grandma Okie because when I was three, my mom always had me dressed in overalls and pigtails and my grandma would always say, "You're Grandma's little Okie."

I would retaliate by saying, "No, you Okie."

Eventually, she was known by all eleven grandkids as Grandma Okie. She came bearing an expensive little stuffed animal called a Furby, a popular toy at that time. My grandma never bought anyone presents—especially expensive ones—so this, indeed, was a momentous moment.

My brother was out of town, playing an intercollegiate football game for Shasta College, a two-year school, but he came to see me around 11:00 p.m. as soon as he heard I was in the hospital. I had aunts and uncles and cousins all came to say their hellos, some bringing me food and others carrying gifts. My room quickly resembled a hospital gift shop, stuffed with items I didn't deserve.

Dr. Freeman stopped by three times a day, eager to exchange a few jokes, and his personable, kind bedside manner was always welcome. A couple of times he'd try not-so-subtle tactics to extract a confession. The green light to go home came after three nights in the hospital, and Dr. Freeman had run out of time. Instead of waiting for me to confess about the poison, he called me out of the closet.

"You know I've had two patients in the past who have tried to kill themselves by eating rat poison."

I raised my eyes to his, feeling amazed at his discovery. My stomach began to turn, and I felt like a deer in the headlights. I had nothing to say; I didn't know what to say.

"I'm supposed to 51/50 anyone who is suicidal."

I just stared at him with my mouth slightly ajar.

"But because of your intelligence, you'd probably just talk your way out of being admitted, and you'd more than likely end up with little or no help and slip through the cracks."

"Probably."

My voice had dwindled to a whisper.

"I don't want that to happen, so I talked to a friend of mine who works here at the hospital. She's a social worker. I told her about what was going on, and she suggested three therapists who she thought would be a good match for you. I want you to choose one."

He handed me a piece of paper with the names of the three therapists and their phone numbers.

"What am I supposed to say when I call?"

"I've called them already, and they all have openings in their schedules, so all you have to do is choose one, then call and tell them what time you can make it."

"Okay."

My voice regained some resonance.

"Promise me that you will call me today after you set up an appointment."

"I promise."

Each response grew stronger in voice.

"Okay then. Today, you are going to be discharged, but you will have to come back into the hospital tonight after school to be hooked up to an IV for more Vitamin K. It should only take about an hour. You'll also have to go to a blood lab every morning for the next seven days to have your blood drawn."

"Why do I have to go every morning?"

"Because there is something they put in rat poison called Coumadin. It's a blood thinner; it's what makes the rats bleed to death."

Then he jokingly added, "Or, in your case, humans."

I giggled at the remark. I thought it was nice that he tried to make the already painful experience less so by joking and laughing with me.

He continued.

"It's fat soluble, which means it's going to take awhile to leave your system. You also will have to take Vitamin K in a pill form twice a day."

That afternoon when I returned home, I got out my list of therapists. First on the list: Marcella.

*That's a dumb name. I'm not talking to someone named Marcella.*

Next on the list was Jaime Freitas. I sat and imagined myself talking to someone named Jaime. It wasn't a bad name, and I liked the way Freitas sounded. Back in the hospital, Dr. Freeman told me that the last person on the list was an older lady and didn't have an opening until next week.

*No, thank you. I'm not going to talk to a granny.*

Jaime was the first person I chose mostly because her available time meshed with mine. I picked up my phone, dialed the number, and waited to hear her voice.

# Chapter 5

## Jaime

"Hello, this is Jaime."

"Uhhh ... Hi. This is Lisa Leachman, and I'm supposed to call you for an appointment. Dr. Freeman said he talked to you."

"Yes, what time do you want to come in?"

I quickly scanned the paper the doctor had given me. He had included a list of possible openings along with the name of each doctor.

"Two o'clock on Wednesday."

"Okay. Do you know where my office is?"

"Yeah."

Dr. Freeman had included the addresses of each doctor on his list, and I knew I could easily find her.

"Then I'll see you on Wednesday."

"Okay, bye."

*Now what?*

Suddenly, I was feeling overwhelmed and scared. My depression had seemed to momentarily subside. Now I was taking medication for whatever was wrong with me and it made me feel a little more real. At least for now.

It was 1:55, and I slowly walked up the red concrete steps to what appeared to be just an old white house. I noticed a small plaque anchored to the wall of the building. Written in gold lettering was *Jaime Freitas, LCSW.*

*This is it.*

I opened the door to a tiny quaint-looking home that had been converted into an office, probably many years ago. To my right were a couple of tan chairs adorned with neutral-colored throw pillows, and to the left of the chairs was a blue couch that also was adorned with matching pillows. A dark oak coffee table with claw feet was centered in the seating area, strewn with magazines: *People, Us Weekly, Sports Illustrated, Highlights for Children,* and a few others that I didn't recognize. Soft classical music was playing in the otherwise quiet office building. I gently closed the door and felt like I should tiptoe so that I wouldn't disturb the stillness of the room.

I stood by the door for a few moments, gathering strength and courage to face a stranger in an alien environment. I had never talked about my feelings to anyone before. I wasn't sure how the words would come out. I've seen therapists in movies before where people are always crying and blowing their nose while a therapist sits in front of them nodding their head, periodically saying, "And how does that make you feel?" always with a sympathetic look on their face, while writing secrets down on their yellow tablets. I smiled thinking about that image.

*I'll never cry like those stupid people, and I'm not going to talk either.*

I was still standing in the entry way when I noticed a young woman maybe in her late twenties. She stepped around the corner and looked at me.

*This can't be her. She's young and pretty, not what I had pictured a therapist to look like.*

"Are you Lisa?"

I shook my head yes.

"Hi, I'm Jaime. Come in."

She motioned for me to come into her office. I immediately noticed her warm welcoming smile, and sparkling brown eyes. She was wearing short overalls that fit her trim, compact figure well. Her curly, black, shoulder-length hair framed her pixie-like face.

Her office was small—tiny, in fact—no bigger than, say, a McDonald's restroom. There was only one window in the office, and it was in the wall furthest from the doorway. Outside of that window, I could see a pit bull at the next-door neighbor's house attacking a black tire swing that was hanging from a branch of cottonwood tree. To my right was a disordered light oak desk and black computer chair with wheels sitting in front of it. A large semihealthy hibiscus plant was sitting beside a white wicker love seat, starving for a drink of water.

The love seat was the obvious place where patients sat. It was adorned by throw pillows and a box of Kleenex, but that's not where I was going to sit. Nope. Only one other option remained. As obvious as the love seat belonged to the patient, the white glider chair with matching ottoman belonged to the therapist.

"Sit anywhere you want," seems like a simply executed privilege, but it's not. Sitting in her chair makes me appear arrogant and bold, a power grabber. If I sit in the love seat next to the Kleenex, then I will be forced to talk about my feelings—not in my plan. So the only other option was to sit in the chair that belonged to the desk. It seemed like the perfect choice—the safest one.

I scanned the room nervously. A college diploma from California State University at Chico hung on the wall, and next to that was a photo of her and with whom I assumed was her infant son. I quickly glanced at her bare ring finger. Already I had learned so much about her. She was most likely a single mom who had her master's degree from a school I knew well, and her desk was a mess.

*Maybe she wasn't so alien after all.*

Now I didn't feel quite so vulnerable because at least I knew a little bit about her.

She sat in the glider chair, which I had correctly assumed was hers. She had to twist to see me because I was almost behind her.

"Why don't you sit over here?"

She motioned for me to sit in the seat with Kleenex on it.

"It's much more comfortable, and I won't get a kink in my neck trying to talk to you."

I liked her smile. Somehow it made me feel a little less intimidated. Not much, but a little.

I knew she would want me to sit in the love seat. Now we were sitting face to face, with only a white ottoman between us. Yet, the scene was very uncomfortable for me. I felt like I was going to crawl out of my skin. I knew I would have to talk to her about eating the poison and why I wanted to die. Even though Dr. Freeman knew I ate the poison, I never had to talk about it. The agony was overwhelming, especially deciding where to start.

Luckily, she talked first.

"Hi."

She smiled trying to break the tension in the air as I sat in the white wicker love seat.

I looked into her brown eyes and nervously smiled, "Hi."

There was a brief moment of silence, probably because she was seeing if I was going to talk, but I didn't. I continued to study the office, noticing nothing different, but it gave me something to do to help ease my discomfort from being there.

"Have you ever been in therapy before?"

I shook my head no.

"Well, let me first tell you a little bit about what I do and what therapy is about."

I stopped looking around the office and returned my eyes and full attention back to her; I was interested in what she had to say.

I already had a pretty good idea of what therapy was about because of my schooling up to that point. In three months, I would be graduating from Simpson University with my bachelor's degree in psychology. I knew that there were as many different methods of counseling as there were breeds of dogs. And just as a dog could be a mutt, so could a therapist. Not many "pure-bred" therapists roamed the earth anymore, which wasn't necessarily a bad thing.

"During therapy sessions we will talk about any concerns you have and also the difficult issues in your life. I can teach you better ways to cope with the difficult issues in your life."

She paused giving me the opportunity to speak, but I didn't have anything to say, so she continued.

"The sessions last about fifty minutes and will usually be once a week—maybe more, maybe less depending on what's going on."

Again she paused.

"I talked to Dr. Freeman this morning. He seems really nice."

"Yeah, he is."

"He told me that he talked to a social worker at the hospital who was setting up eight free sessions for you. So the next eight sessions will be paid by a program through the hospital."

"That was nice of him to do."

"Tell me about your stay at the hospital."

"Didn't Dr. Freeman already tell you?"

"He told me very little."

I began by telling her about the blood in my mouth and then about going to the hospital. By the end of the session, I told her about eating rat poison. It felt good to talk with her. She seemed like a genuinely nice person, and I already felt so much more comfortable with the idea of being there. She didn't feel like a stranger anymore.

The first fifty-five-minute session with Jaime wasn't as painful as I had imagined it would be. I felt, for the first time, a glimmer of hope that I might actually be saved from these terrible feelings that had been overtaking me.

*Maybe she actually can help me.*

"I'd like you to sign this," she told me near the end of the first session. She scribbled quickly on a small sheet of paper and then handed it to me:

*I, Lisa Leachman, promise to call Jaime Freitas or The Help Line if I feel like I*

*am going to harm myself.*

"I can't sign this," I said holding the paper out for her to retrieve.

"Why not?"

I stared at the piece of paper she had handed to me and then looked back at her.

"If I call you when I feel like hurting myself, then you'll call the police, and I'll have to go to mental health. So I won't call you."

"Well, if I thought you were going to kill yourself, then you're right. I would have to call the police, but maybe after talking to me, you would feel better, and I wouldn't have to call them."

She smiled.

Silence. I contemplated what she had just said.

*I wouldn't feel better after talking to her, would I? Could I trust her?*

My thoughts were interrupted.

"Please, sign it. It's just a piece of paper that will protect me if anything happens to you."

I took a chance and scribbled my name at the bottom of the piece of paper.

"That's your signature?"

She smiled.

I chuckled lightly.

"Yeah."

It somewhat resembled scribbles that a two-year-old would have made, but I didn't care.

"Okay, so remember you promised to call me if you feel like you're going to hurt yourself."

I drew a deep breath and shook my head yes.

"Okay."

We made an appointment for the same time the following week.

"Remember, you promised to call me if you start feeling like you're going to hurt yourself."

"I remember."

I stood and began to walk out of her tiny office.

"Bye," she said to me with the same gentle smile with which she had greeted me.

"Bye." I left my first therapy session.

A couple of uneventful days passed before I stumbled back into my familiar dark pit of despair. My stomach ached for food; it had been two days since my last meal. The control of self-starvation was therapeutic. I felt rewarded watching the scale slowly drop over time. But starving myself wasn't enough to numb the all-consuming pain inside my abused body. I needed a razor blade.

I always kept a few box cutters (that I would bring home from my job as a grocery store checker) hidden in my room and in my car just in case I needed a hasty escape from the prison of my mind. Rummaging through my desk drawer, I remembered the contract that I had signed with Jaime. I stopped momentarily. I felt too uncomfortable calling her so I decided to buy some alcohol.

At the local grocery store, I bought a bottle of one-hundred-proof apple schnapps, because it was the easiest to swallow. With bottle in tow, I went for a ten-minute drive to the college.

I loved being at this small community college; it felt soothingly familiar. I had spent the last three years of my life here going to school and playing on three different intercollegiate sports teams: cross country, soccer, and track and field.

The unrelenting pursuit of relief proved impossible to resolve. The peaceful darkness was engulfing me as I sat on the track. The same questions returned.

*Why can't I get better? Why am I such a failure? I wish I was dead.*

The same litany played over and over. I took a long swig of the alcohol, stood up and ran as fast as I could around the track, imagining competitors in the other lanes. My legs burned and my lungs begged for more air, but I didn't stop. I ran until I could no longer stand the pain. Four laps later, I finally slowed to a stop and put my hands on my knees. With sweat dripping off my face, I pulled at the bottom of my white T-shirt and wiped the sweat away. I took a few steps, allowing my heart to slow before I collapsed on the rough all-weather track and cried.

The night air chilled my damp uncovered flesh before I decided to go back to my car. I pulled out my cell phone and dialed Jaime's number. An answering service came online and patched me through to her.

"Hi. What's going on?"

I immediately detected the concern in her voice.

"I need to break the contract I signed."

"Where are you?"

There was just a hint of panic in her otherwise steady tone.

I hesitated.

"Shasta College."

"Why do you need to break the contract?"

I began to cry.

"Life is too hard. I hate it."

"Do you want me to come out there and talk to you?"

Her offer was completely unexpected. It felt good that she cared.

"No, that's okay. You don't need to come."

"I will if you want me to."

"Thanks, but that's okay."

I was still floored by her generous offer of support.

"Then why don't you go home and call me when you get there, okay?"

I agreed to go home.

My mom was still awake watching TV when I got home. I knew she was worried about me and wanted to know what was going on with me, but I didn't want to talk to her. I could see her looking at me from the corner of my eye but didn't stop to talk to her. I knew she wanted to talk to me but was trying her best to give me my space.

"Good night," she said as I shut my bedroom door.

"Good night," I mumbled, closing my door.

"I love you."

With my door closed, I answered, "I love you, too."

The night's calm was a sharp counterpoint to the stormy sea of despair and frustration that roiled inside my body. To release this torrent would have drenched my mom with whatever was left.

My mom always came to my room every night to say good night. And this evening was no different. As usual, I didn't want her to come into my room. I just wanted to be alone. I always wanted to be alone.

"You must not have heard me; I said I love you."

She walked in my room and sat on my bed.

I rolled my eyes and sighed.

"I know I heard, and I said I love you, too."

She brushed a stray hair out of my eyes and tucked it behind my ear. I pushed her hand away from me.

"Good night. Now leave and close my door."

"Why do you hate me so much?"

She was pained as tears glistened in her eyes.

"I don't hate you. I just want you to get out of my room."

She just stared, my rejection taking its painful toll on her maternal concern. She stepped slowly to the door, her eyes still glistening with tears.

"Well I love you very much."

She stood there momentarily and then shut the door behind her.

I grabbed a razor blade hiding in my closet and cut my flesh. Once again my arms and chest would become raw from the hundreds of slashes I would inflict upon myself. To feel and watch the blade rip through my skin was oddly calming. All the anger and anguish I felt was instantly covered up. Besides, I deserved it. I was a horrible human being for making my mom suffer.

I was interrupted by the phone. I grabbed it, realizing that I hadn't called Jaime back.

"Hello."

"Lisa?"

"Yeah"

"Good, you're home."

She sounded relieved.

"I just got home a few minutes ago."

"Well I'm glad you're home. Are you okay?"

"I'm fine."

I stared at the blood, savoring the calming effect of my mutilation. Something terrible had been done, and this was evidence of the punishment. In a strange way my life seemed right again.

"Okay."

Her tone was decidedly skeptical.

"Then I'll see you at our next appointment. But you can call me anytime if you need to."

"Okay."

Days turned into weeks and then disappeared into months as things seemed to only get worse. I started working with Jaime in September, and the holiday season was quickly approaching, and I was feeling even more lonely than usual. I had lost about fifteen pounds since that September, which was a lot for my already thin body. My daily starvation ritual began to intensify once the holidays approached. I kept a journal:

*Monday, November 29, 1999. I haven't eaten anything for three days, but today I had a can of tomato soup and five soda crackers, but I immediately threw up afterwards. I hate myself. I wish I was dead. I miss Jaime.*

*Tuesday, November 30, 1999. I ran two hours today and felt really sick. I took about fifteen laxatives last night and had to sleep in the bathroom I was so sick! I ate one small carrot, and some popcorn with no butter. But I didn't throw up today.*

*Wednesday, December 1, 1999. I just cut myself and got blood all over the carpet, but I don't care. I cut a vein in my hand and the blood squirted like in the movies. I called Jaime and told her, but told her it wouldn't need stitches.*

*Thursday, December 2, 1999. I went to a walk-in clinic to get stitches in my hand this morning. Seven stitches. I guess it was bigger than I thought.*

*December 19, 1999.- I'm really sick, I hate it. I'm never going to get better.*

*January 28, 2000. Well I'm not sure how I'm doing, but I'm getting so fat! I'm never going to eat again. I don't feel like I'm getting better. Instead I feel like I'm getting worse. Some days feel pretty good, but most days I feel like shit. I just don't know how to explain how I feel fine. That's a bunch of shit. I don't feel fine! I feel like shit, I don't "feel" anything. What in the hell am I supposed to be feeling? What am I doing? Who am I? Maybe I'm nobody, just wandering lost in a big, dark, scary forest. I can hear people, but I can't find them; they want to help me—but how? I wish I could find them then I'd be safe and happy. I wonder if I'll ever find them. What if they give up and quit looking for me?*

*February 9, 2000. Jaime wants me to go to mental health tomorrow to check myself in, but I don't know if I'm going to do that because it's really scary for me. It would be okay if Jaime stayed there with me, but of course, she can't. I don't know what I'll do.*

It was December 1999, and Jaime was fielding almost daily phone calls from me with most being fleeting instances of a continuous mode of crisis. I continued my weekly sessions with her and my biweekly appointments with Dr. Freeman. I still had to have my blood drawn every other day, and for a couple of times, I had to be readmitted to the hospital so that I could be hooked up to an IV of Vitamin K. Both Jaime and Dr. Freeman were doing their best to save me from myself despite my seemingly inevitable descent to what seemed sure death.

I was inducing vomiting at least twice a day after eating only small portions of food and eating laxatives like they were candy. I'd go on my daily hour-and-a half run and then ride my bike for a couple of hours. Four nights a week I had school, then would go home and either drink alcohol or take Xanax to fall asleep. The futile search for escape exhausted every bit of physical and mental energy reserve.

I'd lie in bed crying for hours until exhaustion finally would take over. Then I'd wake up to find that only a couple hours had passed, and it would start all over again. The nights seemed to never end. And the following days were even more dreadful. It was as if the clock had become my nemesis. The movement of the day was excruciatingly glacial.

One night I woke up at two, and I saw my mom standing by my dresser just looking at me with a worried expression on her face. I was irritated and confused about why she was lurking over me, and then I realized it wasn't my mom. Turning my night stand light on, I was amazed that my room was empty. No one was there. My heart was pounding, sure that what I saw wasn't a dream. Someone, or rather something, had been standing by my dresser, and it looked just like my mom. My childhood fears of the night had been suddenly resurrected, so I left my light on for the rest of that night and a few nights after that.

Being terrified of the dark is pretty common for many children. I can remember lying in bed as a young girl terrified of all the noises I'd hear and shadows I'd see. It became a nightly routine to sleep with my mom and stepdad, looking for the assuring warmth and safety of being cuddled next to my mom. But one night my mom decided I was too old to be sleeping with them, so I had to face the dark night of endless shadows all alone. The terror was so strong that I could feel cold sweat beading on my body, and I ran to their closed bedroom door, but it wouldn't open. It was locked.

I cried.

"Please let me in," I begged.

"No, you need to go back to bed."

There was no way I was going back to sleep in my room, so I grabbed a small throw blanket off the back of the couch, turned on a lamp, and lay at the foot of their door. I positioned my face as close to the bottom crack of the door as I could, and cried myself to sleep.

Nights became an anticipated fear for many years. As evening approached every day, my heart would begin to pound faster, and fear would start to overwhelm me. As I grew older, my fear of the dark began to slowly subside, but it was only in the last few years that I could be alone in the dark without my heart pounding inside my rib cage.

# Chapter 6

## 51/50

"Merry Christmas."

My twenty-four-year-old brother kissed me on the cheek as he walked in the door. He was handsome with dark hair and green eyes, reminding me of the movie star Josh Hartnett. He was always one of the most popular guys in school; the girls all loved him and begged for his attention.

It wasn't Christmas yet, but every year the extended family would get together to exchange gifts and eat. Aunts, uncles, cousins, grandparents—more than forty people packed into my house to celebrate the holiday. I enjoyed the company of everyone and had a good time. My mom always began preparing for this party a couple of days in advance by cleaning the house and preparing the menu. She loved to cook and prepare different unique side dishes, which would usually go over well. The party lasted three or four hours and went as expected with laughter and good times filling the air—that is, until the party ended.

Once everyone left, I grabbed some leftover chardonnay, conveniently unattended on the kitchen counter, and a piece of chocolate pie. The holiday cheer had been replaced by all-too-familiar pangs of loneliness and depression. I went to my room and took a handful of Xanax, washing them down with the chardonnay and pie. I wasn't doing it with the motive to kill myself. I just wanted to sleep until Jaime came back from her holiday.

The week before, during the regular therapy session, Jaime told me she was going to Europe for vacation. I hated the idea of her leaving and panicked at every slight thought of her temporary disappearance. She introduced me to another therapist.

"While I'm gone, you can call this lady, Stacy, if there is an emergency."

Stacy smiled, looking at me as if she really cared about me (which I knew was false), and with her petite left hand adorned with a diamond ring, she gave me her plain business card, which I reluctantly accepted. The introduction lasted less than two minutes. I didn't really like Stacy. She was old and not too attractive, unlike Jaime, who was young and pretty.

*I'll never call her. I don't trust her, I don't even know her.*

I was angry that Jaime left, creating this crisis of abandonment and desperation. It only took a few minutes for the Xanax to start working, my mind becoming fuzzy and my legs barely supporting my body.

"What's wrong with you? You look like you took a muscle relaxer."

My mom watched as chocolate pie dribbled down my shirt.

"Same as," I slurred, as I continued walking to my room.

I had taken Xanax before, normally prescribed for anxiety. However, it wasn't prescribed for me. I got mine from my college friend Steve. He always gave me handfuls of his pills.

Feeling numb, I collapsed on my bed. My mom came in.

"What did you take?"

Her tone was anxious and urgent, almost shrill.

"Xanax."

"What's Xanax?"

"It helps me sleep."

I closed my eyes.

\* \* \* \*

"Come on, Sweetie. You've got to stay awake."

*What the hell?*

Someone was sticking the most god-awful smelling thing under my nose. I turned to look at my arm as a needle was being pushed into my vein. Feeling nothing, I drifted to sleep, still looking into the eyes of the man torturing me.

"Lisa, come on, Lisa. You've got to stay awake for me. Open your eyes," the man demanded. He shook me slightly and, again, the putrid smell. I coughed, trying to push his hand away from my face.

"Stop it!"

All the pills I had consumed had taken hold of me, and I was no longer in charge.

"I'm sorry, but you need to stay awake."

Straining to keep my eyes open, I was trying to prevent him from using smelling salts on me, but I couldn't. My eyes felt like tiny heavy bricks. Drifting off again, I heard him say to the driver, "Turn the sirens on. She's not responding; her pulse is too low."

Again I was jolted to semiawareness with the sharp aromatic salt. The young paramedic caressed my head, and through the fuzziness, I could detect the compassion in his eyes.

"We're almost there. Just hang on for me."

I felt so cold and desperately wished for a blanket.

"How much more time?" he asked the driver.

I was switching in and out of awareness like a remote control scanning the television stations for something suitable to stay on. People were all around me, and bright lights were everywhere. So much noise and hectic activity.

I opened my eyes to a new scene: a small room with a large window looking out to a large semicircle nurse's station. Two nurses were standing at the foot of my bed, quietly talking. My mind was still fuzzy, and my eyes still felt like tiny heavy bricks.

Suddenly, I sensed an urgent need to pee, and I tried to get up, but wires were sticking to my chest and an IV was in my arm.

"Oh, she's awake."

The female nurse hurried to the side of my bed.

"What do you need?"

The nurse put her hands on my shoulders to keep me from getting up.

"I have to get up," I pleaded, confused and unsure about where I was.

"You can't."

She looked at the male nurse as if she would need his assistance to keep me down.

More angry than confused, I couldn't stand the fact that these two strangers were telling me what I could or couldn't do.

"I have to go pee."

"No, you don't. It just feels like you do."

"What? I think I should know if I have to go to the bathroom."

*What was she talking about?*

"You have a catheter. It just feels like you have to pee, but your bladder is empty."

I didn't know what a catheter was, but it didn't sound good. I felt between my legs and something was there that shouldn't have been there. I furiously pulled on the tube, but it wouldn't budge.

"Don't do that," the male nurse said in a short irritated tone.

Again, I pulled as hard as I could, but the tube wouldn't budge.

"Take it out," I demanded as I continued to pull with all my might.

"I'm sorry, but it needs to stay in. You really should stop pulling on it because you're going to hurt yourself."

The female nurse sounded so much more sympathetic than her male colleague.

"I don't care, I just want it out!"

Feeling trapped and desperate, I began to remove the heart monitor cords from my chest.

"You can't do that. Stop it!" the male nurse yelled.

*If he didn't like me before, now he really didn't like me.*

"I can do whatever I want. And I'm leaving, so take all of this stuff off me now. I know my rights, and I don't have to stay here!"

I glared into the male nurse's eyes, asking for the battle to begin.

In a soothingly calm, almost motherly, voice, the female nurse stepped forward, moving her colleague to the side.

"If I remove the catheter and put you on a portable heart monitor, will you stay?"

I felt triumphant.

"Yes, thank you."

The nurse suddenly seemed to be my best friend. Both of us knew that I would never have been able to leave. I could barely hold my eyes open and my legs felt like Jell-O.

She did what she said she would, and once she finished, I immediately fell back to sleep.

The next morning seemed to come quickly; it was already ten o'clock. My mind still felt a little fuzzy but much less than the night before. I looked around at my surroundings.

*I've never been in this part of the hospital before.*

It appeared that all of the patients' rooms formed a circle around the nurses' station.

I lay my head back down, as a young female nurse walked into the room.

"Good morning, how are you feeling?"

She checked the fluid in my IV bags.

"Fine, thank you."

I watched as she lifted the empty bag off its perch and replaced it.

"What's in the IV bags?"

I knew one was just a water solution, but I didn't know what the other bag contained.

"We had to give you potassium," she said as she finished replacing the bags.

"Your body was critically low in potassium, and if a person's body becomes too low in potassium, there's a risk of them going into cardiac failure."

I said nothing and just stared at her. I didn't care if I had a heart attack. In fact, I'd welcome it with open arms.

"You know, a lot of times when a young person has such low levels of potassium, it's most likely because they're inducing vomiting a lot."

I shrugged my shoulders at the nurse's comment and looked away much as if a rich person would do in dismissing a servant from the room. She took the cue and left, passing my brother in the doorway.

He had two of his friends in tow: both I knew well enough to consider brothers. I knew James and Steve from high school. They were my brother's best friends and were at my house as much as my brother was. Steve was a Wintu Indian with close connections to the local casino Win River. He was handsome and knew it. James stood six foot four and could envelope anybody with a bear-sized hug. All three were stars on the high school football team. They smiled, each greeting me with a kiss.

My brother didn't approach me. He stood at the foot of my bed, disapprovingly shaking his head.

"Do you have any fucking clue what you put mom through last night?"

I could sense the nervous smile on my face, now burning red with embarrassment from his comment. I looked away from him and made eye contact with Steve as if asking for help.

"She was up all night crying. What are you doing? What the fuck do you think you're doing?"

I knew he wasn't mad. He was scared and felt out of control in finding a way to help me, but his words stung hard and deeply.

Finally Steve stepped in.

"Fuck, Troy, lay off. She's laying in a hospital bed. Yell at her when you get home."

He smiled and winked at me.

Troy drew in a deep breath of air and started over.

"You must be pretty embarrassed."

"No. Why would I be?"

"Don't you remember what happened last night? You acted like a fool."

"I did not!"

Now I was feeling indignant.

*Why did he have to show he cared about me in such a harsh way?*

He didn't know anything about what I felt like inside. No one did except me. I was burning up from the inside out, my lungs searing with every attempted breath. As I fought back tears, the fire inside me raged, causing my chest to burn in torturous pain.

"Do you fuckin' remember them cutting off all your clothes and putting a tube down your throat?"

I didn't believe him. I would have remembered something like that. I swallowed to see if my throat was sore.

"They had oxygen on you, and you kept fighting to take it off."

He paused for a moment, as if summoning strength to continue scolding.

"Doctors and nurses had to physically hold you down to shove the tube down your throat."

Tears now welled in his eyes as he listed the details of the events as vividly and clearly as possible.

I tried to stay emotionally disconnected, but once again my eyes began to fill with tears.

*Don't cry, you stupid fat pig. You are worthless. I hate you! You have no right to even breathe the same air as everyone else.*

These internal reinforcers successfully disconnected me from the emotional pain being inflicted with each stark, clear word out of my brother's mouth.

I stared at my brother, my glacial insulation icy and solid. I felt completely numb, and words seemed to float over my head. Nothing would have bothered me now.

The tension broke as he let out a chuckle.

"Well, do you remember talking to Dad?"

"No, why? What did I say?"

I smiled with him as his chuckle morphed into a full-throated laugh.

"It was classic. Dad came up to you and said 'I bet you won't do that again.' And then you said in almost a growl ..."

He paused to control his laugh again.

"'What do you know? You're only thirty-five, and you don't even have a job.' I had to turn away to hide my face because I was laughing."

"Well, what did Dad do?"

"Nothing, he just turned away laughing and said, 'Well she's right about one thing, I don't have a job, and I wish I was only thirty-five."

I laughed. But in the back of my mind I felt hurt by my Dad's detachment, his lack of concern.

*Why doesn't he love me? He's my dad. Why doesn't he love me, if even only a little bit?*

My brother's words about our dad confirmed my feelings of being unlovable and worthless.

"Lisa," a nurse interrupted.

"I'm going to take the IV out of your arm, and then you'll be able to leave as soon as the discharge paperwork is finished. The doctor who treated you is on his way up to talk to you."

I was relieved at the thought of going home. My brother, with his two friends, left when the nurse came in, so now I just sat and waited to be released.

"Lisa?"

An average-looking man wearing a white overcoat stepped into the doorway of my room. I looked at him. He reminded me of the young kid doctor from my favorite TV show in the late eighties, *Doogie Howser, MD,* with his boyish face and sandy blonde hair. The difference between them was his toothpick body, which made his head look too big for his neck to support.

"Because of the situation, I have to 51/50 you."

His tone was austere, cold, and unfriendly.

"But I wasn't trying to kill myself!" I pleaded with him.

"The paramedics should be here any minute to drive you to mental health."

He paused for a brief moment.

"If you cause any problems, we'll have the police escort you there."

He turned and walked out.

As he walked out, I saw two paramedics standing at the nurse's station with a wheelchair. A new nurse whom I hadn't seen before came to my room and asked if I was ready. Without answering, I just got up and walked to the waiting paramedics.

"I can walk. Do I have to sit in that thing?"

He looked at the nurse who nodded.

"You can walk if you want."

Once in the ambulance, my mood switched to playful.

"Could we turn on the sirens?"

The driver responded, switched them on briefly, and I smiled at the wailing sound. I made small talk for the short five-minute drive to the county mental health hospital.

"So how's your morning been?" I asked the thirty-something paramedic as if we were long lost buddies.

"Oh, pretty good so far. But my shift is just getting started, so we will see."

He smiled and talked briefly with the driver.

"You like doing this kind of work?"

"Yeah, I love it. It's my life."

I didn't necessarily believe him because of his brief hesitation and small nervous movements before answering my question. But I really didn't care about what he had to say. The only true thing on my mind was how I was going to keep myself from being admitted to the county mental health hospital.

As we pulled up to the hospital, I felt completely disconnected and numb, my head and body still a little fuzzy and weak from the previous night. I wasn't worried about being admitted because I knew I would be able to talk my way out of my predicament. I felt confident if not arrogant, self-assured about my intellectual superiority.

With the ambulance coming to a stop, I looked out the window, remembering many years ago asking my mom what this place was. She told me that it used to be a regular county hospital back in the sixties before it was converted into a purely mental health facility. Back then it used to be clean, new, and well maintained. A huge decorative fountain sat in the middle of the courtyard with a wooden gazebo to its far left. A large concrete walkway led visitors to the few steps they would take before entering. Everything was surrounded by lush green shrubs trimmed regularly to keep it neat, and the gazebo was adorned with different types of wildflowers.

However, this hospital was no longer the beauty it had once been. It was overrun with shrubbery and weeds, and the fountain was dried up, no longer functional. Cracks in the cement were filled with persistent weeds trying to find their way to the surface. Once it was switched to a mental health hospital, very little money went into fixing it up. It just continued to rot away until its present appearance: a sad undermaintained mess.

I was escorted into the old rundown hospital; the overwhelming odor of "old" filled my nose, like the back lot for a bad, cheaply made horror film. The scene was dark and scary with hallways going everywhere but leading nowhere. It was too cold for the T-shirt I was wearing. Much like a prospective home buyer checking out a potential fixer-upper, I was disgusted at the dirty paper that had started to peel from the wall. My escort, however, was no chatty real-estate agent.

*What the hell kind of place is this?*

There were disheveled crazy people sitting in a small room waiting to be seen by the psychiatrist. Luckily, that's not where I was going to be left sitting. Instead I was put into a small room to wait alone for a counselor. It didn't take long for me to take in my new surroundings, just four concrete walls that were painted in an undistinguished white and an equally bleak concrete floor. I sat in an uncomfortable brown metal foldout chair with a long sterile-looking table in front of me. A couple of matching chairs completed the setting. The décor was as harsh and stark as imaginable in even a bitter minimalist setting. Boredom was instant.

Luckily, I didn't have to sit too long before a man, probably in his middle thirties walked into the room. I smiled at him as he entered. I looked confidently into his blue eyes until he looked away. That was how I measured a person's strength. The longer they held eye contact, the stronger they were. As for this man, he looked away almost immediately. For that reason I knew that I would happily be leaving soon. He held what I confidently assumed was a list of stock questions for newcomers. I was worried for nothing. I smiled.

The questions were not at all surprising to me, and I knew how to answer them to get what I wanted, which was to get out of there. I talked in a controlled, gentle—if not childlike—voice, masking any stress from difficult questions with humor.

"I'm not suicidal. I just wanted to sleep. That's why I took the Xanax and sleeping pills. But under no circumstances did I want to die."

I leaned forward, staring deeply into his green almond-shaped eyes, intent on making him believe the responses to his standard questions.

"I'm a little depressed, but I'm working with a therapist already."

I knew I had to give him something substantial in order to establish solid credibility. This was exactly what he wanted to hear, and, after only a few minutes, he seemed satisfied with my presentation and decided to let me go home.

# Chapter 7

## The Gun

At college, I met a guy, maybe ten years older than me. His weight definitely not proportional to his height (six feet), Steve always talked about needing to be on a diet, often admitting he would make himself vomit after eating. His face was a chubby round, framed by natural dirty-blond hair. When he wasn't talking about dieting, he seemed to obsess about death and murder.

"You know," he began one evening after class as he stared at the forty-foot clock tower, "I could sit up there with my rifle and just start shooting everyone, and by the time they found me, you would all be dead."

I just stared at him, trying to discern if he was credulous or if he merely intended to shock whoever would listen.

After watching me study him for a few seconds, he smiled and shoved me.

"Don't be stupid, Lisa. I wouldn't really do it."

"Ya, you would because you're a crazy psycho."

I smiled and pushed him back.

"Why don't you get braces? Your teeth are really crooked."

"You're a bitch. I don't even know why I like you."

We both laughed as we found our cars in the school parking lot.

I don't remember when I confided in Steve, but we became fast friends. From the first day of class, we sat together at the same table, and, within weeks, we were chatting constantly about death. We had one major thing in common—we were obsessed—inexplicably and eerily fascinated—by thoughts of death.

One week in class, he decided to confide in me.

"Once I put a loaded shotgun in my mouth and pulled the trigger, but nothing happened. The gun didn't fire."

"You probably had a few too many Xanax, and just thought you pulled the trigger. Are you sure you had bullets in it?"

I laughed a little. He shoved me, rolling his eyes and laughed.

"No, there were bullets in it. It just didn't fire."

He paused, waiting for me to absorb the impact of these revelations.

"I sobbed afterwards, feeling that there must be a purpose for me in this world."

After a brief pause, I asked him, "Why are you so fucked up? What happened to you?"

Steve hesitated for a moment, scanning his anguished cerebral computer for just the right words.

"It's my stepdad. He's a murderer; he just hasn't been caught yet. He was violent and abusive to everyone in my family, especially me. Since I was the oldest, I'd try to protect my mom and the younger kids by physically intervening, so I got the worst of his shit. There were a lot of times that he would tie me to a tree outside and put the dog's bowl of water beside me. He would force me to sleep outside like a mutt. That's how he liked to refer to me—as the mutt."

Steve stopped talking, and I could see the haunted look on his face. He didn't say anything more, and I didn't ask. I hoped he realized how very much I sympathized and cared. Some feelings just go beyond words.

A few weeks later, sitting in the back row of the class, I whispered to Steve next to me.

"Steve, give me one of your guns."

He just laughed at me. "SHHH!"

"I'm serious. Please, will you?"

"What? You want to shoot yourself?"

"Yeah, let me borrow your gun."

"What the fuck, Lisa? I won't get it back because the police will confiscate it. No, I like my guns."

A few moments passed as he pondered my burdensome request.

"You can go buy yourself a gun."

That was something I had thought of in the past, but I knew I would have to have a gun permit in order to buy one, which would take too long. I would have to wait several months just for a gun safety class to begin and then spend three hours every Saturday for six weeks.

"It takes too long to get a permit. And I want a gun right now."

My tone was insistent, stubborn, final. He grinned.

"Why? You won't do it"?

His words stung with his tone of mockery.

"Well, I guess we'll just have to wait and see, huh?"

I was irritated by his absolute smugness. He didn't know me. He fueled the fire in my body, and my competitive drive came out in full force. I squared my shoulders to his, looked him in the eye, and smiled.

"Help me buy one and find out."

"Fine, I'll help you get a permit today then."

His smile seemed chillingly familiar. Perhaps he had sensed accurately my resolution.

We took off to a local Wal-Mart. It was a short five-minute drive.

Getting out of his red Bronco, I asked, "What do I say?"

"I'll do most of the talking. You just go along with it."

That sounded easy enough. We walked through the front doors of the store, acknowledging the Wal-Mart greeter.

"Hello, do you need a basket?" the balding white-haired man asked with a fake smile on his face. He looked tired and bored.

I smiled back, "No, thank you."

"That's going to be your job in twenty years," I said to Steve once we were out of the old man's hearing range.

"Funny... at least I'll have a job."

We laughed.

I was giddy as we walked straight to the back of the store to the hunting and fishing department. Finally, I was going to get a gun. Now the end was within reach, and a wave of self-satisfaction filled me. All pain and despair were finally going to end.

Steve talked first, just like we had previously planned.

"Hi, this is my little sister, and she needs a hunting license."

"Yeah, sure. Do you have proof of completing a hunter's safety course?"

"I took the class a long time ago, but I lost the paperwork."

"Well, how about an old hunting permit?"

I just shook my head no and shrugged my shoulders.

"Well, legally, I can't give you a hunting permit without some kind of proof that you took a gun safety course."

"I'll let you see mine if you want."

Steve pulled his own hunting license.

"We took the course together a long time ago, maybe five, six years ago."

The man looked over Steve's license and nodded.

"Okay, but next time—remember to bring some kind of proof."

He seemed reluctant, but, trusting our story, he got a permit out of a locked drawer and handed it to me to complete.

As I wrote my name and address, I began to daydream about the gun I was going to be buying in less than an hour. Once again, I was feeling giddy.

After I completed filling out the permit, I handed it back to the man behind the counter who was making small talk with Steve.

"I'm sorry. I'll keep better track of my permit next time."

He just smiled in return.

I already had thirty dollars sitting on the counter to pay for the permit. He took the money then signed the permit and stapled the receipt to it and gave it back to me.

"You guys have a good day."

He smiled then turned his attention to the next customer in line.

Steve and I walked away from the counter.

"Wow! That was really easy."

We both smiled at each other, proud of how easy the challenge actually was.

"I told you."

Arriving at the gun shop was exciting, but at the same time, my stomach was churning with excitement-induced acidity. The warm sun was beating down on my face as I left the truck.

"What if they know what I'm going to do with the gun?"

He rolled his eyes at me.

"Don't be stupid."

He led me straight back to the gun counter walking past all of the odds and ends things people bring into a hawk store: radios, TVs, VCRs, jewelry, and guns.

"Hi. Can I help you guys?"

I was more than willing to let Steve handle the overweight scruffy-looking man at the counter.

"Yeah, she needs to buy a gun."

"Well, what kinda' gun you lookin' for?"

"I don't really know. I guess something that would kill a deer."

"Okay, how about this forty-five. It would easily kill a deer."

He took the gun out from behind the glass counter and placed it in my hands.

"Good, because I don't want to have to shoot it twice."

I smirked and looked at Steve. The gun felt cold to touch and was much heavier than I had imagined it would be.

"How much?" Steve asked for me.

"It's three-hundred forty-nine dollars and ninety-nine cents."

I smiled at his precise announcement.

"Okay, I'll take it."

No hesitation.

"Now you know there is a ten-day waiting period before you can take the gun home." He shuffled through folders to get all the necessary paperwork for me to fill out.

"I know."

I completed the paperwork and gave him the cash from my pocket.

"Okay, I'll call you in a few days when it's ready to be picked up."

Steve and I both thanked him and left the store.

\* \* \* \* \*

That evening, I was still excited about my new purchase. I was sitting in my bedroom playing a game on my computer when my phone rang.

"Hello?"

"What are you doing?"

It was Jaime. Her normally calm voice now was thick with anger.

I stammered, but because of the tone of her voice, I knew that it was the wrong answer.

"No. What are you thinking?"

"I don't know."

I was now sounding like a child with a taboo that had just been discovered by her mother. I was a little confused about why she was so angry because there was no way she could have known about the gun, but at the same time, I knew that's what she was talking about. To be on the safe side, I wasn't going to reveal anything about the gun until I knew for sure why she was so upset.

"You bought a gun!"

She didn't give me a chance to answer before she continued on, and no way was I going to try to interrupt her.

"Are you planning on shooting yourself? Where is it?"

I was just stammering on the other end of the line.

*How did she find out? It had only been a few hours ago that I bought it.*

She took a deep breath releasing the tension before she spoke again.

"Where is the gun, Lisa?"

"I don't have it yet."

I turned off the volume on the TV so that I could hear her better and so that I could concentrate on how I needed to respond. Jaime was formidable as a therapist and as a person.

"What do you mean you don't have it yet?"

It was obvious she didn't believe me.

"There's a ten-day waiting period. I just bought it today."

I could hear her urgent tone subsiding. I needed to know.

"How did you know I bought a gun?"

"Some guy named Steve called and left a message on my voice mail. He said you bought a gun."

She took a deep breath.

"How on earth were you able to buy a gun anyway without a permit?"

"It was easy."

Then I continued to tell her exactly how easy it was to get the permit and then onward to the Olde West Store to purchase the gun.

"I'm calling the store and telling them not to sell you the gun." It wasn't a question but a fact.

"But I already paid for it."

I was protesting like a kid whose mother said she could not have a toy. I was resigned to the fact that she was going to call the store.

"I'll call you right back."

I knew that I wouldn't have to wait. About ten minutes later, she called to say that I could go down to the store with my receipt and get my money back.

"What did you say to him?"

"Not much. I just told him that you shouldn't be buying a gun and asked if you could get your money back."

I was irritated. The carefully orchestrated exercise had been dashed within the space of about fifteen minutes.

"How about I meet you down at the store tomorrow morning at eleven thirty so that you can get your money back?"

"I don't really want to."

Now, I was like a sulking teenager.

"That's okay. I'll meet you tomorrow at the Olde West at eleven thirty."

She was sounding a little more chipper now that this ordeal was coming to a conclusion.

"Fine!"

I said good-bye and hung up immediately.

* * * *

The next morning, I met her at the store to retrieve my money. It was another beautiful day in Redding; a light breeze was blowing my hair into my face as we walked into the store. I felt awkward about getting the refund. The same man who sold me the gun was there, and he was now doing the return. He just stared, making me feel a bit uncomfortable.

*Maybe he was waiting for me to change my mind about getting a refund. Not with Jaime there standing by my side.*

She did all the talking and all the work. I just stood silently. He quickly completed the refund. No questions; no need to explain.

As we walked out of the store, Jaime smiled.

"Now, you should go shopping."

"Yeah, maybe."

I felt a little sad about losing my gun, but that feeling was almost zeroed out by the perception that somebody was looking out for my interest and safety. Even though I had wanted to use the gun to end my life, it felt good to know that Jaime really cared whether I lived or died.

"This time, you should just stay at the mall."

Jaime's smile seemed to brighten even more.

I returned her smile. It was as if she could melt a glacier with her smile, and indeed, it was heartwarming. I felt surprisingly good as I left the store.

We walked together into the parking lot, and as we found our cars, she looked at me with large luminous eyes above a sweet smile.

"Be safe. And I'll see you later."

With my own eyes glazed over, I just smiled and nodded as I climbed into my blue Geo Storm.

I felt dizzy from the extreme emotions pulling me in every direction: total hate and despair one moment, then love and compassion the next. It felt as if I were being pulled apart at the seams, but in reality, the love I felt was almost certainly the glue that was holding me together.

# Chapter 8

## The Psychiatric Hospital

Several weeks had passed since the gun return, and there were no major incidents beside the normal cutting and starving myself. I continued to feel smothered by complete darkness, except for the small glimmer of light I would feel whenever I talked to Jaime. I loved being with her even if it was only for one hour a week. It was the one thing I anticipated enthusiastically every week.

Our sessions mainly revolved around crisis intervention, because I always seemed to be in that mode. So most of what we talked about was focused on the present:

"What were you feeling when you cut yourself?" she would ask. "What happened just now to cause you to feel like dying?"

Delving into my past to attempt to sort out the cause of my extreme self-hate would have to wait until I was a little more emotionally stable.

Jaime was going out of town again but only for a few days this time. Like always, when she was going out of town, she would make me promise to go to mental health if I felt like I was going to hurt myself. And I would always tell her that I would, knowing that I would never go.

This weekend was different. I had begun the night drinking alone until my sister and cousin visited. Hearing the front door open, I left my room to investigate who the intruders were.

"Hey, what's up?" my younger cousin by three years asked as she walked up to me and hugged her tiny arms around my shoulders.

"Hey Johnie, what are you doing here?" I hugged her back, noticing that her light blonde hair was only a few inches away from touching her butt.

Johnie was strikingly beautiful with the body you would expect to see on a runway at a high-end fashion show. But she didn't see herself in that same light. She saw herself as gangly and ugly.

"Nothing. I was just out and about and decided to drop by to say hi."

She had been tiny even when she was a baby and had almost died until the doctors finally figured out what was wrong with her. She was severely glucose intolerant.

My sister was already in the kitchen grabbing a Keystone Light from the fridge when Johnie and I finished greeting each other.

We gathered around the small light-oak breakfast nook table and played several different card games. My favorite was crazy eights. After about an hour—near ten—the alcohol I had drunk once again awakened the tumultuous raging sea of emotions.

I left the table and went to my room, sat on my bed, and began to silently sob into my pillow for no reason in particular. In order to numb this new flood of emotions, I grabbed the razor blade that I kept hidden in my computer desk drawer and made fresh cuts over the not-so-old ones from two nights earlier.

My sister walked into my room and immediately noticed the blood on my clothes.

"Did you call Jaime?"

"I tried, and I can't get a hold of her."

"Then you should go to mental health."

I tried to call Jaime several more times but wasn't able to get through to her, so I eventually gave into my sister's request, and we left.

When we arrived at the mental health hospital, my face was puffy, streaked with tears. It was close to eleven, which was after hours, so my sister pushed the buzzer next to the front door. I began to regret agreeing to go when a man opened the door for us.

"Follow me."

He led us down the darkened hall to the admittance room. The old building was even scarier this time, with the bustling pace of the day gone. No one roamed the halls; the lights were turned off in most places, giving the old building the atmosphere one would see in one of those slasher films. I walked close to my sister, fearing that we would be the surprise victims of some anonymous killer.

We finally made it to the brightly lit inpatient ward of the hospital. The man took out his bulky ring of keys and fumbled with them until finding the right one to unlock the large white steel door that led to the same sterile room I was in last time. Nothing changed. It was the same large table surrounded by the same eight chairs that I remembered seeing the first time. I sat in one of the folding metal chairs closest to the exit door, even though there was no chance of escape because I was now a prisoner locked in this small sterile room. My sister sat next to me in her own metal chair.

"I'll go get the admittance counselor, and he'll be right in."

The man locked the door.

"I don't really want to stay," I said to my sister.

"It will be good for you, and you'll probably get out tomorrow, anyway."

My sister was doing her limited best to be reassuring.

"But it's nasty here. Disgusting."

She didn't disagree but instead nodded her head in agreement.

A different man, not much younger than the man who escorted me down the hall, walked into the sterile room, holding a white clipboard. Silver streaked his dark hair that was messily styled. He was wearing a pair of khaki slacks and a white button-up shirt that looked good with his dark complexion.

He sat down in a metal chair that matched my own with the clipboard in hand and began reading off questions for me to answer.

"So, what's the problem?" he asked in a far-from-compassionate tone.

Tears streaked my face, and my eyes were red from crying for so long. I just stared at him without answering his simple question.

"She's suicidal," my sister jumped in to take the lead and continued, "she needs to be admitted."

Knowing the hospital didn't admit people when they were drunk, my sister would have to plead her case to get me in there.

"Well, we usually won't accept someone when they're drunk."

And I was noticeably drunk, definitely unable to speak without slurring my words.

"She will kill herself if you don't admit her. Look."

She pulled up my shirt sleeves to reveal the blanket of fresh cuts covering my arms.

"Oh. Well, I guess we can put her in her own room for tonight until she sobers up."

Once he saw the cuts, he had a change of heart and quickly made the decision to admit me.

"Well, okay, let's go inside. We have to fill out some paperwork before I can let you go to bed."

He stood up and signaled to my sister that it was time for her to go.

I said good-bye to my sister and was led through a new door that took me inside the main section of the inpatient unit to the dining area. Because it was so late, all the patients were already in bed. Despite the staff, the place seemed quieter than my bedroom at home.

"Before I can let you go to bed, I need you to sign some papers to admit yourself, and because you have to be 51/50ed, you won't be able to purchase a gun for five years."

"Why am I being 51/50ed? I willingly came here."

My annoyance rattled the unsettled calm in the ward.

"I know. I'm sorry, but I have to in order to admit you."

"Fine."

I signed the papers sitting in front of me.

"Okay, now the nurse is going to go through your things just to make sure you don't have anything that you can hurt yourself with."

I handed my bag over to a definitely unfriendly chubby woman and watched as she took everything, one by one, out of my bag.

"I don't think you need this."

She held up a razor blade she had found.

"Oops. I forgot that was in there."

"You always keep razor blades in your bag?"

"Yeah."

I didn't offer her any more information, and she didn't seem to care.

She pulled out two of my schoolbooks that I had packed and began thumbing through the pages, searching for contraband. I was extremely annoyed by how thorough she was being, because it was taking forever and I just wanted to sleep.

Once my bag had been inspected, I was escorted into a tiny private room.

"I get my own room?"

"Just for tonight."

She simply had no strain or speck of sympathy or compassion in her eyes or in her voice or in her bearing. She turned to me just as she was about to close the door.

"I'll give you ten minutes before coming back to shut off the lights."

I didn't respond or even look up at her. I didn't like her. Iwanted to go back to the safety of my home, my bed. My thoughts didn't have too long to dance in my head before the alcohol in my system took over, and I passed out on the bed.

It seemed like I had just fallen to sleep when I was awakened by a nurse who was about to draw my blood. I was used to my daily blood draws, so I didn't even wince when the needle found its target. I smiled at the nurse as she waited for the vial to fill with my blood. She returned the smile.

"Here, you hold the cotton while I put the Band-Aid on your arm."

\* \* \* \* \*

The morning hours passed as I sat in the safety of my room. I wasn't going to leave the room until I needed to. Breakfast came, and I barely bothered to look at what was on the plate because I hated to eat breakfast especially when it was watery eggs. After sitting for an hour smelling the putrid eggs, a dark-haired man finally came in to take my plate away.

"Are you done with this?"

"Yeah."

He took it away with no further questions.

Lunch came two hours later: a turkey sandwich, some carrot sticks, and apple juice. It didn't look bad, but now I was proving a point. I wasn't eating until I could go home.

Extreme boredom was taking over and an overwhelming sense of regret for agreeing to admit myself was beginning to eat at me when finally a short woman in her early forties came into my room.

"You have an appointment with the psychologist at two-thirty today."

She was too curt with her words. And didn't bother to say anything else before she turned and walked out again.

*Thank God. Maybe I'll be able to go home.*

\* \* \* \*

It was finally two-thirty, for my appointment with Dr. Hass, a clinical psychologist. Earlier that day, I had asked a nurse when I could leave, and she told me that the doctor would determine that. So I knew that I'd have to pour on the charm. The door to his office was open, and so I just made a little noise to get his attention.

"Are you Lisa?"

"Yes," I said smiling

I quickly scanned the room. It was ordinary and nothing stood out except that it needed more light. The only light gracing the room came from a window on the opposite wall from the door. Papers were scattered on the top of his large cherry wood desk. Only one picture was in the room, and the back of the frame faced me, so I couldn't see who was in it.

He pointed to a wooden oak chair in front of his desk.

"Well, please come in and have a seat."

I was smiling, charming. I was going to be the perfect guest.

"So tell me. Why are you here?"

"I really want to go home. I was feeling a little depressed last night, but it's just because I had been drinking. I feel a lot better now."

"Well, what would you be doing out there that you're not doing in here?"

*What a stupid question!*

All sorts of sarcastic replies came flooding into my brain, and I fought hard to remain polite and composed.

*Do you want a do-over so that you can actually put a little thought into your question before opening your mouth? Whoever said there was no such thing as a stupid question was wrong, because that was a stupid question.*

I bit my tongue and replied, "Well, for one, I could go outside instead of being cooped up in here all day long. I need to run and exercise. It makes me feel better."

He didn't answer. Instead he picked up a tan medical folder and started reading what I assumed was my ever-growing file that, by now, was at least an inch thick.

"Well, it says here that you haven't eaten any meals, and you haven't taken a shower, and you're not participating in any of the group therapy sessions."

I was shocked. I had no idea they were monitoring me and watching everything I was doing.

"Well I'm not eating the food because it looks disgusting."

I paused momentarily.

"Would you eat it?"

He looked at me, clearly skeptical and knowing.

"I eat here all of the time. The food is actually pretty good."

I was hardly going to give credence to any of his replies.

"I'm not going to take a shower here because it's nasty."

"Do you feel like you're better than everyone here?"

The question took me a little off guard.

"No, I'm just not going to get completely undressed to take a shower where anyone—man or woman—can walk in because the doors don't lock."

I took a moment.

"And besides, it's not like I'm doing any strenuous exercise. I've been sitting on the bed all day long. I don't stink."

I looked at him, trying to scan for any signals.

"I … can I go home today? If you let me leave, I'll take a shower when I get home."

I smiled as I finished the last sentence.

He didn't answer, but he did smile back at me.

"I'm not going to kill myself, I promise. I'm fine."

He just stared at me. It was a clinical game of poker. He was indeed a hard player.

"I spoke to your therapist today."

I was panic-stricken, trying desperately not to reveal my shock.

*Damn!*

I knew at that moment I wouldn't be going home because she would campaign to keep me in there, especially because she was out of town.

"What did she say?"

I asked even though I knew what the answer would be.

"She thinks it would be a good idea for you to stay here for the full seventy-two hours, if not longer. If we think its necessary, we can keep you here for two weeks."

"NO WAY! I don't need to be in here. Please let me go home today."

My voice choked with tears.

"I don't think you need to be here for seventy-two hours, but I think it would be a good idea for you to stay another night."

Before I could add even a single note of protest, he continued.

"And if you start eating and participating in the group therapy sessions, then I'll think about letting you go home tomorrow afternoon."

I didn't say anything to him. I bolted out of the chair and left his office.

*I can't believe this. I have to stay locked up in this hellhole another night.*

Back in the room, a staff member stopped me.

"You need to get your stuff together because you're moving into the main bedroom."

I followed him down the barren hall to my new quarters. I was totally disgusted when I saw the fifteen metal-framed beds side by side in the room. I just stared blankly at him, not knowing what to think or say.

"You can pick any bed you want. It's only you and one other person in here."

His tone hinted that he was trying unsuccessfully to make the situation appear better than what it really was.

I chose a bed close to the door, just in case I needed a quick escape from some crazy person who might attack me in the middle of the night. I put my bag down on the bed and decided to take the doctor's advice: I needed to start interacting with people. So I began pacing the hallway partly out of boredom and partly so that the nurses would see me and write in my chart that I was out of my room.

The hours passed excruciatingly slowly; I could sense the relentless pulse of the second and minute hands on the clock. I'd look at the clock anticipating an hour had gone by when in fact only twenty minutes had passed. Later in the day, more people were being admitted. First, a lady with long straggly black hair. She was much shorter than me but quite a bit older, probably in her early forties. She seemed normal enough as I watched her being admitted and then as her bags were being examined. It was my only entertainment.

The second person arrived shortly after her. He was a fairly tall, average-looking guy in his thirties. He seemed unusually nice and too passive as he greeted everyone with a smile, but he would never look them in the eye. And when he talked to the staff, he always said, "Yes, ma'am" and "Yes, sir."

*It's an act. Just like me and just like most of the people here. Doing and saying what they think other people want to see and hear.*

Finally, I watched the window darken with the growing twilight. It was 6:00 p.m., and dinner was being served. I knew I would have to eat, so I grabbed my plate and sat at a table by myself. I stared at the contents on my plate: some sort of pasta, a dinner roll, and some broccoli and carrots. I began running my fork through the pasta, searching for any sign of contamination or disgusting flaw. It actually didn't look too bad, and it smelled good. I cautiously tasted it and was surprised to find that it tasted good, though I would never have admitted it publicly. I took my time grazing over the food, knowing there was little if anything else to do. I ate enough so that the nurses would indicate in my chart that I had eaten most of my dinner.

I walked the halls for the rest of the evening until they said it was time for bed.

*Time for bed?*

It was only 9:00 p.m., but I didn't complain. There wasn't anything better to do anyway. (I had a book, but the lights had to be out in fifteen minutes, so there was no point in getting it out.)

It seemed like hours before I finally drifted off to sleep, only to be rudely awakened every hour by a nurse who would open the door and point her laser light at me. I had fallen asleep again, but this time I was awakened by the light being turned on. *What the hell?*

My sole neighbor was punching into the air.

"I'm going to kill you, fucker. I hate my dad. I hate my brother."

She rambled about her dad and boxed unproductively into the air. It was amusing at first, but then I was kind of scared about sharing a room with this crazy girl.

I got out of bed and tried to sneak by her without being seen. I walked down the darkened hall to the nurse station.

"What do you want?"

The female nurse's tone was curt; obviously irritated that I was interrupting the conversation she was having with other staff members.

"The girl in my room won't turn the light off, and she's boxing in the air saying she's going to kill her dad."

"Okay, we'll be right there."

They seemed a little nicer now that they realized I wasn't going to cause any problems.

Back at my room, a male nurse came in and told her to go to bed and if she didn't comply she'd have to sleep out in the hall again.

*Again? Take her now. Make her sleep in the hall. I don't want to sleep with the crazy girl. I thought I was locked in here for my safety, not to be murdered in my sleep by some psycho girl. Shit. Now I'm never going to be able to sleep.*

Thoughts of being murdered by this girl continued on in my head until I finally found comfort in the realization that maybe I wasn't so crazy after all.

Afterwards, the night passed without any further incidents, and crazy girl fell to sleep, and I eventually did, too.

Morning came too soon, but there was no mandatory time that we had to get out of bed, so I slept as long as I could without missing breakfast, which was over at 10:00 a.m. Even though normally I never ate breakfast, I had to today—for the nurses.

After breakfast, they told me that I had to see the psychiatrist, and then he would determine if I could go home that day. I was furious. I already thought the psychologist I had seen yesterday was sending me home today.

I walked into his office prepared to do and say whatever I needed to get out of there. I made eye contact with a short Asian-looking man with a thick accent.

"Come in. Sit."

He pointed to a black leather chair.

I surveyed the room and quickly noticed that his walls were covered almost like wallpaper in frames of all of his achievements and awards, most of which were for seemingly mundane things. It was definite overkill.

*He really thinks highly of himself.*

I smiled, but he didn't. He immediately began talking.

"So you want to go home today?"

I had to strain to make out his words because of his thick accent.

"Yes, I'm fine. I don't need to be here. I would be much better off if I could be home doing things."

I could tell he was in a hurry; he wasn't really interested in what I was saying.

"Well, it says here," he said as he looked down at my chart, "that your therapist thinks you should stay for a few more days."

"She's only a therapist. You're a doctor. Do I seem suicidal to you?"

I was prepared to say anything at that point even if I had to inflate his already obviously well-stoked ego to get discharged.

He just looked at me for a second, not saying a word and then nodded in agreement with me.

*Wow. This is going to be much easier than I first expected.*

I wasn't surprised when he told me he was going to sign my release papers for that day. I knew he was too busy to deal with someone like me. After all, I had learned early on that appearances do mean everything. If I dressed and looked nice and talked as if I were well educated, then more times than not I could talk my way out of most anything. After all, I must not be too much of a threat if I'm attractive and educated—at least that's what they thought.

The rest of the morning passed quickly once I knew I would be leaving. At one, I was surprised and shocked to see my sister walking through the door. She looked like an older slightly larger version of me. I was so happy to see a familiar face; I walked up to her and gave her a hug. We sat at the nearest table, which was a plain, cheap, metal folding table that one would normally expect to see leaning against the wall of someone's garage collecting dust and spider webs. Four brown metal fold-up chairs sat at the table waiting for the unfortunate people who had to sit in them.

My sister and I were two of the unfortunate people. We both sat in the uncomfortable brown chairs and immediately began people watching, trying to discern why they were there and then diagnose each of them as either a psycho or an alcoholic. Not many people were there, so our game ended rather quickly—after only fifteen minutes.

"I'm going home today."

"When?"

"I don't know, but the psychiatrist said he was signing the release papers, so I can leave."

"Well, that's good."

"Tell me about it. This place sucks. I hate it here."

"Yeah, it's kind of gross."

For the next hour, we doodled on plain white paper with some crayons in the entertainment/group room. I don't know what was so entertaining about the unrelentingly plain room. The only things were crayons and white paper to decorate. Two beige couches sat on opposite walls facing each other; they looked as if they were from the Salvation Army, sporting a few wear holes and smashed cushions. A couple of un-matching chairs were interspersed throughout the coldly institutional room.

We continued to talk about the other patients until the allotted one-hour visit was over.

"Visiting time's over." Someone was yelling outside in the hall.

All five of the guests packed up their belongings and proceeded to leave. My sister lingered as long as she could until a woman finally had to tell her that she had to leave.

I went to the nurse's station.

"When can I leave? Dr. Piae said I could go home today."

The nurse looked at the chart and back at me.

"I don't see in your chart that you're going home."

"But he told me I could go home."

"Well, he's probably still here. Let me call him and check, okay?"

"Okay, thanks."

Another hour passed, and I still had not heard anything from the nurse, so I approached her again.

"Did you get ahold of the doctor?"

"Oh, yeah. You won't be leaving until after dinner."

"Why can't I leave now?"

"I don't know. That's just what he said."

It was now 2:30 p.m., and every passing hour felt like three, and I had to wait yet another four hours to go home. I sat on my bed thumbing through a *People* magazine until the pages began to look worn.

"Lisa! Lisa! Is there a Lisa Leachman here? LISA!!!" A voice yelled down the halls.

"What the hell is that?" I said loudly.

I poked my head out my door, and it was the long black-haired lady who had been admitted the night before. She saw me look out the door.

"The phone."

She dropped the phone, leaving it dangling from its cord.

I hadn't even noticed the phone before that moment. I walked over and picked it up.

"Hello?"
It was Jaime's familiar steady, calm tone.
"Hi!"
I was excited to hear her voice.
"How are you doing?"
"I hate it here, and I'm leaving because it's nasty and scary."
"It's not that bad."
"Yes, it is."
My tone was adamant.
"No it's not. I've been there lots of times before."
"Well, you only had to stay for an hour, and you didn't have to sleep here."
I took on a scolding tone. Jaime, however, was not concerned.
"That's true, but I think it's great that you're there.
I rolled my eyes to no one in particular.
"I'm going home tonight."
"If you stay longer, I can come visit you."
*Hmmm, she's not a good briber.*
"No, thanks. I'll visit you at your office."
"Okay."
I could hear the smile in her voice.
"I'm on a pay phone outside of the store with my son, and it's really cold."
"Why are you on a pay phone?"
"The battery on my cell phone is dead, and I had to stop to get food for my son's fish. I hope it's still alive."
"Who is it, Mommy?" I could hear a little boy's voice in the background.
"It's my friend."
"Oh, where is she?"
"Why do you want to know?"
"Just tell him I'm in a hallway," I told Jaime.
"She's in a hallway," Jaime said to him.
"Oh."
That seemed to quench his desire for information or else he just got bored of the conversation and already had moved on to his next passing target of interest.

"Just a minute, Johnny, come back over here. I have to go. He's cold, and we need to get home to feed the poor fish."

She sounded worn out.

"Okay," I answered.

"I'll talk to you tomorrow, okay?"

"Okay, bye."

"Bye."

And the line went dead.

Once again talking with Jaime had effectively calmed me. I walked the halls, recounting our phone conversation, feeling peaceful and happy.

The nurse was right, and I was discharged after dinner. I walked out of the hospital and took in a deep shot of the fresh, bracing, chilled air. I went to my car as fast as I could and then locked the doors, in case the hospital staff changed its mind. It never felt so good to be sitting in my car. Free.

Chapter 9: Drunk in Public Arrest

After being admitted into the county inpatient mental health hospital, I was more terrified than ever that the day might come when I might have to return. But that didn't stop me from continuing to hurt myself. I became almost addicted to cutting myself, escaping from the emotional turmoil I felt inside. The Prozac that Dr. Freeman had prescribed for my depression wasn't helping at all, so I just quit taking it. My blood was back to normal, so I no longer had to have blood draws and sporadic IV drips of the blood-thickening agent. I felt saddened that I would no longer be seeing Dr. Freeman. He was always kind and compassionate toward me. I would miss him.

With fresh feelings of abandonment, I drove to the hospital parking garage and found a space on the top tier of the structure. I just sat in my car with a bottle of one-hundred-proof apple schnapps, rerunning the same litany in my mind of this intractable feeling of unfairness. Mired at the bottom where there was not even a shred of hope that things would improve.

*I've spent a lot of time here over the last few months.*

I tipped the bottle back and took a long gulp. It burned as it always did with my first few swigs as they worked their way into my long-tortured stomach, I immediately felt the falsely assuring warmth of the cheap booze.

It didn't take long before my lips and nose began to feel numb from the alcohol. I stumbled out of my car and walked to the rail, looking up reverently at the night sky, which was spackled with stars. Four stories below were open fields, and I thought about the possibility of jumping.

*Not far enough of a drop to do the job,* I thought as I finished off the bottle of alcohol then threw as far as I could and waited for the crash of the breaking bottle.

It was eight-thirty, and by then I was totally numb. I couldn't feel my fingers or toes. My legs were unsteady as I walked down the steps of the parking garage and into the front entrance doors of the hospital. There were only a couple of people walking around: an old balding janitor cleaning out the garbage cans, and a man and woman holding hands as they exited the building. No one paid me any attention, which was good because my eyes were bloodshot from crying and my legs quivered.

I pushed the down arrow button and the elevator doors opened immediately. I stepped over the threshold and pushed *B* for the basement. I was motionless, staring at the lit *B* button as a distant memory forced itself into my consciousness.

\* \* \* \* \*

"I'm going to race you down in this one," I yelled to my mom as I ran to an elevator across the hall. I was a skinny nine-year-old with long blonde hair.

"Okay, then I'll see you in a second."

I pushed the *1* button and the doors immediately opened; with one last look at my mom, I waved and then jumped into my elevator.

I watched as my doors slowly closed and saw the other door close, too.

"Hi."

My heart jumped as I turned toward the stranger's voice. I hadn't seen him as I entered the elevator just moments before. He must have been standing if not hiding in a corner. He looked like one of the men from that movie *Deliverance*. He wasn't too tall but was definitely older because he was beginning to bald.

"Want to hold my hand?" He grinned and stretched his hand out toward me.

I shook my head no and squeezed my little body as far as I could into the corner, not taking my eyes off him.

*Please open. Why isn't the door opening?*

"Come over here and hold my hand."

He became more demanding and placed his other hand over a pocket knife that had been cached underneath his flannel jacket.

Fear shot through my young body as I gathered whatever courage I could to step toward the door to push the *L* button. Tears flooded my eyes, and I was getting panicky when suddenly, as if by a miracle, the doors opened. I shot out the doors as fast as my legs could carry me and ran into a man who was wearing a long white overcoat.

I looked up at him unable to speak.

"Are you okay?" The look on his face showed true concern and worry.

I fought back my tears and nodded.

He must not have believed me because he asked, "Are you lost?"

I didn't answer, I just turned and walked away, desperate to find my mom. I needed my mom.

"Lisa!"

I turned, knowing immediately that it was my mom. I ran to her, finally able to release the tears that I had been holding in for so long.

"Where have you been? I was worried sick about you?"

She was a little angry until she noticed my distraught state.

Her anger turned to concern as she bent down to embrace my now trembling body.

"Is this your daughter?" The doctor had followed me because of his concern.

My mom nodded.

"What happened?"

I proceeded by telling the entire story. I had been missing for almost ten minutes.

*Ding!*

The elevator doors opened, and I shuddered as I left the empty elevator trying to shake the memory and the extreme feelings of helplessness that I had felt as a nine-year-old little girl.

\* \* \* \*

I walked down a quiet hall until I came to the cafeteria. In a far corner beside a public restroom, a phone hung on the plain white wall. I picked up the tan receiver and called Jaime.

"Hello."

"Hi, it's Lisa." I said weeping.

"Where are you?"

We were running through the familiar questions and answers. The most important question always popped up.

"Are you going to kill yourself?"

"No."

I sat on the floor with the phone pressed to my ear as a group of people came walking out of a meeting room. I looked toward the ground, so they wouldn't see my condition, but it didn't work. Their eyes scanned me carefully and thoroughly with the degree of concern so common to clinicians. As they passed, a security guard came up to me.

"Did you call the police?" I asked Jaime.

"No, why are the police there?"

"I'm not sure. I think it's a security guard."

"Are you okay?" The short, overweight security guard asked, carrying the same look of concern. He stood at the other side of the hall staring at me with his hands on his hips, not daring to come too close as if I had been infected with the plague.

"Yeah, I'm fine. Thank you."

I looked straight into his beady green eyes, trying to reassure him that I was fine with the confidence of my stare.

He stood for a second before turning away to go back down the hall. By then I was beginning to get worried. I didn't want to go back to the county mental hospital. Only a few minutes had passed when the same security guard came back down the hall, but this time he was being followed by two city police officers. They both walked with the same nonexpressive look on their faces.

My heart began to beat faster as they grew closer to me. I knew they were there for me when I saw the security guard point at me.

"Shit. That security guard is coming back with two police officers," I said to Jaime.

"What?"

She sounded genuinely surprised.

"Call me right back, okay?"

The officers approached me before I could answer her.

"Who are you talking to?" One of the officers asked. He was so stocky and short that it seemed like he didn't have a neck.

I didn't want to answer, but I felt like I had no other choice.

"My therapist."

"Well, you'll have to call him back."

He took the tan phone from my hands.

"It's not a him. It's a her."

My voice was thick with anger as I unsuccessfully tried to choke back my tears.

"I haven't done anything wrong."

"Have you been drinking alcohol tonight?"

"Just a little bit."

I lied.

When we arrived at the lobby, two other police officers were there standing by the doors. I couldn't believe there were four officers there for such a stupid thing. The other officer escorted me to a soft blue floral chair and asked me to sit. I found that this man was much friendlier than the one with no neck, so I began aligning myself with him.

"Just call me Officer Jerry," he said with a kind smile. He was overwhelmingly tall but not frighteningly so. He had more of a protective energy about him.

I was sitting on the back of the chair with my feet in the seat while talking and joking around with Officer Jerry, who sat in a matching blue floral chair directly in front of me.

The no-neck officer approached me; obviously angry for my lack of concern given my current situation because he glared coldly at me. Once he was standing in front of me blocking my view of Officer Jerry, he growled, commanding me to sit in the chair the proper way.

"Why? It's not hurting anything," I said sincerely. "My shoes are off."

"SIT."

He was angry and obviously didn't like me.

"And put your shoes back on."

I looked at Officer Jerry, who was still smiling. I didn't move.

*Who was this guy anyway? I haven't done anything wrong, and I'm being treated like a criminal. I can sit here however I want.*

When I didn't sit the way he had requested, the no-neck officer walked over, getting his handcuffs out with one hand and grabbing my arm with the other. He forced me off the chair and put my arms behind my back then proceeded to handcuff me.

"Now sit!" He ordered.

I glared defiantly at him.

"You can't handcuff me. I didn't do anything wrong."

He ignored me and walked away to the empty receptionist desk where one of his fellow officers was on the phone.

I listened to the man talking on the phone about me.

"Who's he talking to?" I asked to anyone who would listen to me.

Officer Jerry, who I had befriended, walked over to where I was sitting.

"He's talking to your therapist," he said in almost a whisper.

I had no idea how she got through to talk to the police at the hospital, but I didn't care. I didn't want to go to jail, and I knew she would help me. I prayed she could help me.

"I want to talk to her, please," I said to the officer talking on the phone.

"Shut up and sit back down," the no-neck officer growled.

I sat and slipped my feet through my arms to get the handcuffs to the front of my body. Then I stood up.

"Let me talk to her, now!"

A fire was growing inside of me. I felt like a prisoner who did nothing wrong and no one would listen to me. The resolve was surprising. Defeat was not my option.

The mean no-neck officer walked over to me.

"Did you do that?"

"Yeah."

It was time to call the bluff.

"If you do it again, and you don't stay in your seat with your mouth shut, I'm going to shackle you."

He put the cuffs back behind me, but this time he cinched them as tight as they could go without cutting off my circulation.

I tried again to get my legs through, but this time I couldn't, and when I tried, I accidentally tightened them even more. Now they were painfully cutting into my wrists. I looked at one of the officers who had been standing at the doorway, clearly there only to act as a backup should the need arise.

"Please, will you loosen these? They're hurting me."

He looked at me for a second and then to the no-neck officer.

"I will only if you promise to behave."

"I promise. I just wanted to talk to Jaime," I told him as he was loosening my cuffs.

"Maybe when he's finished talking to her," he said and then walked back to his post by the door.

I took my seat and listened to what the officer was saying to Jaime and tried to reconstruct the play-by-play. I could tell it was a heated conversation because he raised his voice, almost shouting at her.

"Hey, quit yelling at her!" I yelled to the mean no-neck officer. At that point, I had nothing to lose. He already hated me.

He turned around in anger.

"Shut your mouth or I'm going to put you in the back of my car."

I rolled my eyes at him but didn't say anything else.

By what was being said, I could tell that Jaime was trying to talk the officers into taking me to the mental health hospital instead of arresting me. But the officer talking to her said that they couldn't take me there because I was drunk and that he would have to take me to the jail.

After a few minutes, the conversation was over, and he hung up the phone. Jaime had lost.

"Hey, you said I could talk to her!" I yelled.

However, no one paid any attention to me. The mean no-neck officer walked up to me and grabbed my arm again, but this time he was walking me to his car, which was parked with the other two police cruisers in front of the hospital entrance doors.

I looked him straight in the eye.

"Aren't you going to read me my rights?"

"No."

"You're an incompetent human being!"

Oblivious to my protest, he took control, placing me in the back of his cruiser. He didn't seem moved by my threats.

"I'm going to sue you."

He settled into the driver's seat and told me to be quiet. Of course, I didn't listen to him. I lay down on the black plastic seat and rambled on about how mean he was and that he should read up on the laws to become better informed.

"Just shut your mouth; we're almost there," he said, obviously growing tired of all my negative remarks that apparently only fueled the fire even more.

"No. I have every legal right to talk. Have you ever heard of something called the freedom of speech?"

He ignored my remark and tuned me out for the rest of the two-minute drive.

The police station was only two miles at most from the hospital, so it only took a couple of minutes to arrive. We pulled into a garage reserved for police vehicles, and he parked beside an older man with short graying hair who was sitting at a desk. I was seated in a gray metal chair placed at the head of the desk. The older officer had a gold nameplate attached to his blue button-up uniform shirt indicating he was Captain Anderson.

He briefly looked up from his forms that he had been filling out to greet Officer No-Neck.

"Who have you got here?"

As I looked into his blue eyes, fresh tears began to run down my face.

He smiled at me with true compassion in his eyes.

"What's wrong?"

His tone seemed almost grandfatherly, with no hint of anger that a father might show in a similar situation.

I dissolved into sobs, my whole body trembling. Captain Anderson seemed to listen with sincere empathy. I finally regained my breath.

"He's being very mean to me."

The captain looked to his side where the mean officer stood.

"Officer Shaw, are you being mean to this girl?"

He said something that I couldn't make out.

Crying harder now, I said to Officer Anderson, "Now I'm going to be put in a cell with a bunch of fat lesbians, and they're going to try to rape me."

The captain chuckled almost as if a parent had heard something similar from a child who was being reprimanded for doing something wrong.

"No, I'm going to give you your very own cell, and it even has a nice little mat for you to lie on."

"You are?" I asked in disbelief.

"Yep."

He smiled again.

Relieved, I stopped crying. It didn't take long for Captain Anderson to complete the paperwork. And before I knew it, I was being escorted down a hallway to have my mug shot and fingerprints taken. Once the humiliation of being booked was over, I was placed in a small cell with a cushioned mat on the floor. I was exhausted, and the alcohol I had consumed earlier wasn't helping things.

I lay down on the mat and closed my eyes. My head was spinning as I passed out listening to a man in the cell next to mine.

"Fuck, what the hell. Isn't anyone listening to me?"

"Quit cussing!" I yelled to him.

"Oh sorry, ma'am."

He apparently thought it was an officer's voice he had heard.

I smiled at this modicum of power I still had, and then unable to hold my eyes open any longer, I fell asleep after being at the station for nearly an hour and a half.

* * * *

"Wake up! Time to go."

A middle-aged officer who I didn't recognize was standing in the doorway of my cell.

"What time is it?" I asked, rubbing my eyes and yawning.

"Six a.m. Time for you to go."

He walked me and two men to the door of freedom and then turned around to walk away.

"Aren't you going to drive me back to my car?"

"Get a taxi," he told me.

"I don't have any money."

"Not my problem."

Not only was he curt in his tone, but his look suggested that I must have been completely nuts to even think of asking him for a ride.

"But, you brought me here."

Desperate, I was terrified of the dark, and didn't want to walk the two miles back to my car.

"Do you want to stay?" He asked as he touched his handcuffs on his belt.

Rolling my eyes, I turned and walked out the door. Because it was still so dark outside and I was disoriented, I had no idea which direction to go. So I started to walk aimlessly around until I found a street I recognized—where Jaime's office was located.

With my bearings identified, I ran as fast as possible down the street. I looked over at Jaime's empty office as I ran, noticing how different it looked with no one there. I wished she was there now.

From Jaime's office, I was a little less than halfway there, and I was quickly running out of streetlights. I was running for my life in a bad part of town surrounded by total darkness. On my right, was a solid wall of bushes, and I was no longer on the sidewalk, just a dirt path that followed closely to the main road. Looking ahead, my heart dropped when I noticed that I was quickly approaching an area where I would have to run without any light at all for about three hundred yards. I was imagining all sorts of horrible, scary things waiting for me in the dark bushes.

Entering the "dark zone," I slowed to a walk when I noticed a shadowed figure that seemed to appear out of nowhere only fifteen feet in front of me. My heart was already beating fast from running, but now it was in overdrive.

I remembered watching something on *20/20* several years earlier that talked about a study done with prison inmates. They had the inmates watch videos of women walking to their cars in dark parking lots in which they were supposed to choose the most likely women that they would attack. It was only the women who kept there eyes downcast and walked timidly to their cars that the inmates pointed out to be potential victims.

With the *20/20* program fresh on my mind, I looked straight at him and continued to walk boldly as if having no fear whatsoever. We both held each other's stare until eventually he looked to the ground. I felt much better once he broke the stare, and once I knew he was about fifty feet away, I began to run again—this time faster than ever.

I was finally approaching streetlights again, but there also was a hellish hill. Maybe if I hadn't just slept on the floor in a jail cell and if I wasn't hungover, I could have made it to the top without walking, but halfway up the hill, my legs were burning with fatigue, begging me to stop. I ignored the pain as long as I could, and then I surrendered and began walking. At the top of the steep hill was the hospital: my long-awaited destination.

I was out of breath and thirsty as I climbed into the safety of my car, locked my doors, and collapsed in the seat.

*Thank God, that's over.*

# Chapter 10

## Guardian Hospital

It had only been a few weeks since getting out of jail when Jaime told me she had to move away, after which I decided to climb that one-hundred-foot power pole. Jaime was only trying to save me from myself when I sat motionless and speechless in her office as she convinced me to enter Guardian Hospital's outpatient program for six weeks.

"Please, Lisa, will you do it for me."

This time, no head shaking. I looked up at her, and that was all. It was the green light she was waiting for, and there was no time to let another spell of silence reverse the course of what she had fought for with unrelenting discipline.

As we walked out of her office, I looked in her eyes, searching for even a small reminder of assurance I would need to use as some small source of inspiration in the upcoming months. We exchanged smiles as we left each other. I followed her little maroon four-door sedan for the three-mile trek to Guardian Hospital, my new temporary home.

I watched as she pulled into a space so that I could park as close to her as possible. She left her car and walked toward me as I shut the engine off.

*I don't want to get out of my car; I don't want to be here.*

Alone, I wouldn't have followed through. But Jaime's own gentle resolve was enough for me to gather myself to walk into the hospital.

As we walked through the large sliding doors, I noticed how large the building was. To my left was a large seating area full of tan leather couches and matching chairs. A large vase full of fresh mixed wildflowers sat on a small cherry wood corner table beside one of the couches. It was a still-new building: less than ten years old, recent enough to have that smell of newness. This place wasn't as bad as I had first imagined.

Straight ahead was a young woman sitting behind a large receptionist's desk with a phone cradled awkwardly between her chin and shoulder as she fumbled for some apparent object. She hung up the phone as Jaime and I approached the desk. She looked up and smiled at us, pushing her glasses up higher onto her pointy nose.

"Hi, Lisa Leachman is here," Jaime told her.

"Okay, have a seat and someone will be with you in a couple of minutes."

We walked to the only tan leather couch in the room and sat, waiting for whoever was going to come take me away. Not even Jaime's calm assurances mollified my nerves as a young attractive man approached us after we had waited only five minutes. He was maybe in his late twenties, with sandy blond hair, and he stood at least a head above me. I looked to Jaime for strength as she stood to greet him.

"Hi, this is Lisa." Jaime said, pointing her right hand toward me.

"Hi."

My voice was meek, barely loud enough. I fixed my eyes on Jaime, avoiding every attempt at eye contact with the young man.

"Hi. I'm Jason, the intake counselor."

He smiled as he shook Jaime's hand and then mine. He asked us to follow him.

I felt completely relieved when Jaime walked with me.

*She isn't leaving.*

I smiled at her as we were ushered into a small room. We sat side by side on a small couch as the intake counselor, clipboard in hand, sat in front of us in a chair that matched the couch.

"Have you ever experienced a significant loss?"

"My dog Sassy disappeared when I was really little. I think she was dognapped."

I smiled like a kid trying to be cute and sassy. Jaime looked at me like a mother, chiding me for being flippant.

"Lisa."

"What? It's true. I loved her. I cried nonstop for at least a week. I would stand at the window in the front of our double-wide trailer home, crying, waiting for Sassy to come home."

"Okay."

Jaime obviously did not believe that I was being serious.

From that point on, she answered most of the questions for me. It seemed like I was going to be the subject of a biography: Where have you worked and for how long? What high school did you go to and did you graduate? Did you go to college? Are your parents still married? Do you have siblings?

*Is he ever going to shut up? This is ridiculous.*

After a grueling twenty minutes, he finally finished the questions, and the young man tucked away his pen and stood up. He smiled at Jaime and thanked her for helping, then turned his attention towards me.

"I'll take you down to the treatment room."

I looked at Jaime nervously, not saying anything, but my face clearly suggested that I was not ready for this.

She smiled and said, "It's alright. I can't stay any longer because I've got a client coming in five minutes, but you'll be fine."

I watched as she walked down the hall into the lobby until I could no longer see her.

"Are you ready?" the man asked.

"Yes."

We followed the same hall Jaime had crossed just seconds before.

*As ready as I'll ever be.*

Instead of going into the lobby as Jaime had done, we turned to the right and walked down a second hall that wasn't too long—maybe twenty-five feet. We passed several offices with people handling miscellaneous tasks, some working on their computers, some on the phone, and others doing paperwork.

We made another right turn and walked down yet another hallway; this one was at least twice as long as the first. On the left was a large cafeteria with doors leading to a small designated smoking area that had a weeping willow tree planted right in the center that was bordered by a wooden bench. On the right were several closed doors with no hint of human life inside. A few large pictures hung on the walls: all were of different landscapes. My favorite was of a large snow-capped mountain in front of a beautiful sunset.

*This building is much larger than it looks from the outside.*

"Here we are," he said, opening one of the closed doors on the right side of the hall. We walked into the outpatient psychotherapy area.

The surroundings were small but comfortable. The room was like an incubator containing three smaller offices—for the psychiatrist, head nurse, and three counselors. A fourth room, the largest by far, was where all the counseling took place.

A short hallway of about fifteen feet connected all the rooms: two on the right side, one on the left side, and the fourth was where the hallway dead ended.

I was introduced to Dr. Ballard, whose tiny office was the first one we came to on the right side of the miniature hall. His office looked as if it had been a walk–in closet at one time. He was a mature sixty-year-old graying man who stood up from behind his desk and shook my hand. He stood probably six-foot-three, and he seemed well proportioned. His smile seemed as big and warm as his appearance. He was like a gentle giant who radiated unmistakable kindness. Immediately, I knew I would like him.

Next I was introduced to Karen, the nurse, who was probably in her midfifties and sported short, curly brown hair streaked with gray that framed her thin, smallish face. She was standing at the calendar board that broadcast the ward's daily activities. She, too, smiled kindly and shook my hand

The man who escorted me into the mini office looked at me and said, "Well, Karen is going to take over from here."

"Okay," Once again I found my barely audible meek voice.

Karen smiled at me again.

"Well since the day is almost over, I'm not going to have you start until tomorrow. But first I'll give you a little tour of where you'll be spending most of your time."

"That sounds great."

She started first by pointing out the four rooms that I had just passed. We couldn't go into the main room because she didn't want to disrupt the therapy session that was in progress.

It wasn't what I had expected. We left the closed door leading into the main hallway as she continued giving me a tour of where I would be spending the majority of my days. I felt a strange sense of peace. Now I wanted to get better more than anything in the world.

*Who knows? Maybe being here will cure me.*

I had already walked by everything that she was showing me, but I didn't say anything. We went into the cafeteria, which was about half the size of a basketball court full of cafeteria tables and chairs. Two vending machines sat pushed up against the wall: one was full of junk food and the other contained sodas and water. She then pointed to the door that led outside to the weeping willow, and told me that it was the designated smoking area, even though there was a large sign on the door indicating as much.

"Well, that's that," Karen said, ending the five-minute tour.

*I guess I won't be getting lost here.*

Karen's obvious indications had made me a bit sarcastic.

"We'll start at eight-forty-five tomorrow morning and, please, DON'T be late."

The next morning I woke up before my alarm clock. I was nervous, thinking about meeting the other patients in the program. I sighed as I rolled out of bed, saying out loud, "I hope they're nice."

I arrived at the hospital at eight-thirty. I always have hated being late so I'd started a little earlier than I'd really needed to, just in case I ran into any traffic problems or unexpected snags. I sat in my car listening to a local soft rock music station for a few minutes trying to get the butterflies out of my stomach.

Eight-thirty-nine.

"I hate this," I mumbled, stepping out of my car. I made my way to the door of the mini-office and closed my eyes as I opened the door, took a deep breath, and entered.

I shut the door behind me, and almost directly to my right was Dr. Ballard's small office. He was sitting at his desk doing paperwork. He looked up and smiled as he heard me enter.

"Good morning, Lisa," he said as I walked past his open door.

"Good morning," I replied, smiling. I continued to walk down the short carpeted hall to where Karen was standing. She seemed casual, relaxed, drinking a cup of coffee from a plain white mug.

"Do you want a cup of coffee?"

I wrinkled my nose in disgust, shaking my head

"Okay, you can go in and have a seat anywhere you want."

I surveyed the room. There were two beige couches backed against two adjoining walls. One love seat and two chairs matching the couches were placed in a vain attempt to shape an arc. An oversized coffee table, littered with miscellaneous magazines sat in the center of the crude circular arc. In front of it all sat one wheeled wooden chair, apparently the counselor's seat.

At the opposite end was a table, much like the kind in a cafeteria, pushed flush up to the wall, holding stacks of papers and a computer. Three brown metal fold-up chairs were placed in front of it. A couch with a forgettable floral design seemed to be the only relief from the otherwise nondescript institutional feel of the room. I sat in one of the brown fold-up chairs and waited as the group members filed in individually.

The first to enter was a shabby-looking mountain man, maybe in his early forties. He had brown medium-length hair pulled back in a ponytail. A full beard and mustache covered half of his face. I could smell the strong odor of cheap cigarette smoke as he took a seat at the couch. Grabbing a magazine off the coffee table without looking at its cover, he looked at me and smiled, acknowledging my presence with a slight nod. Even this brief encounter was enough to see scars of the obvious disappointment of his life, an aggregated sense of pain and sadness burned into his eyes. Without saying a word, he turned away and began thumbing without any true sense of interest through his magazine.

Barely a minute later, two people walked in together. They were talking and laughing as if they had known each other for years. One was a middle-aged man, perhaps no older than his early or middle fifties. He carried himself as if he was a businessman or some professional. He was clean cut and wore large glasses that accentuated his overall nerdish appearance. The other was a woman in her fifties. She had an ordinary but classy-looking black leather purse hanging over her shoulder. Her short black hair, which looked like it had recently been permed, was neatly groomed. She was a small-framed woman barely five-feet-two, wearing nice black slacks and a button-up blouse. Both stopped talking when they noticed me, an obvious intruder to their apparently tight clique.

It was now exactly eight-forty-five. The group leader entered promptly. His long hippy-looking hair had gone totally gray, but he didn't look older than forty-eight, which didn't seem old enough for a person to be completely gray. Like the others, he had a warm, peaceful presence about him. He immediately looked at me.

"Please sit in the 'circle furniture.'"

Another person—wearing a black long flowing dress that covered her overweight body—walked into the room, puffing, anxiously asking if she was late. Her face resembled that of a horse. It was really long, fitting for a horse but not a human. Her black pixie-cut hair complemented the horse look well.

"No, come in. We haven't started yet." His warm demeanor was intact.

For the first time, I was extremely uncomfortable.

*I am so much younger than everyone else here.*

The leader started the session.

"Good morning. We have a new member in our group. This is Lisa."

All eyes were now on me, and I could feel the heat forming in my cheeks as they reddened with embarrassment. They knew their roles and began introducing themselves.

The business man spoke first.

"Good morning, Lisa. I'm Dan."

He smiled. My uneasiness was clearly palpable. He added, "It's not too bad. We're all pretty nice ... except for him."

He looked at the mountain man and everyone laughed, including the mountain man.

Dan's verbal touch immediately eased my tension, and I smiled.

The mountain man introduced himself.

"I'm Dwayne."

His voice was soft, and he seemed painfully shy, not at all what I had expected from him.

The two women were sitting on a couch together. The short, black-haired woman introduced herself first.

"I'm Janice. Welcome."

She smiled warmly then looked toward the other woman.

"Hi."

The other woman was having a hard time looking me in the eye. She seemed skittish and uncomfortable in her own skin. She was overweight; even the long plain black billowing dress did not conceal her large frame. She was quite homely, with cropped short black straight hair that was buzzed at the neck.

"My name is Lynn."

She looked first at the group leader and then at me.

"Okay now," the group leader began to speak.

"My name is Al, and I'll be facilitating the groups."

Al talked a few minutes about what we'd be doing every day for the next six weeks.

"I'll be greeting the group every morning for about fifteen minutes to 'warm' everyone up for the upcoming day. Then the next forty-five minutes will be an informational time with Karen, the nurse, who will be teaching us about different aspects of mental illness. After that, we'll have a fifteen-minute break. From ten to eleven-thirty, you'll be back with me for what we call group psychotherapy. Eleven-thirty to one is lunch break, and lunch will be provided in the cafeteria. One to two is addiction therapy for those that need it, and those that don't will have exercise therapy. After another fifteen-minute break, you'll be back with me again for the last hour and a half."

I climbed into my car at the end of the first day feeling exhausted, like finishing the first day on a new job. At least it wasn't as bad as I had imagined it would be. Everyone was extremely nice and because of the large age gap between me and everybody else, they quickly became almost parental, offering me advice. But I didn't mind.

Dr. Ballard gave me three samples of medication to begin taking as soon as I got home.

"Ambien is for sleeping. Wellbutrin and Lexapro are both antidepressants, but they both work differently in the brain."

I liked Dr. Ballard a lot. He was like a great big protective grandpa, the kind who adores all of his grandchildren and gives them what their parents won't. He certainly wasn't like either of my two grandpas, both alcoholics and sexual perverts.

During the first week, I made fast friends with all of the other group members. Each one had his or her unique pain and suffering. Lynn, the homely woman in the plain black dress, was schizophrenic, always asking me if what she was seeing was really there. Both men were drug addicts in recovery and suffering from depression. Janice was going through some sort of midlife crisis and seemed hopelessly depressed.

On Friday, Dr. Ballard asked me if I had seen the doctor.

"For what? I'm not sick."

"It's just part of our normal admissions process. Everyone gets a checkup. It's no big deal."

He then turned to Karen, who had been standing in the hall.

"Why hasn't she seen the doctor yet?"

"I'm not sure, but he's not here today, so I'll put her on his calendar for Monday." She immediately scrawled a note on the large dry-erase calendar hanging on the wall.

Because it was our lunch hour, I left the 'mini office' and went into the cafeteria. My new friends were all outside smoking, which was something I despised. I grabbed an apple and started to stroll around when Dr. Ballard, standing at the entrance of the 'mini office,' called out to me.

"Lisa, come here a second. I want to introduce you to somebody."

A tall, large-framed man who looked to be in his midforties was standing next to Dr. Ballard. He was dressed in black slacks and a black, short-sleeved dress shirt. His shoulders were so big that he looked like a body builder. True to form like every other staff member, he smiled as he greeted me when Dr. Ballard introduced us.

"This is Lisa Leachman. It's her first week in the program."

He turned to me and added, "This is Greg White, the doctor you're going to see on Monday."

"Hi." I put my hand out to formally greet him.

Dr. Ballard continued talking about me for a couple of minutes, building me up as if I were this great intelligent person. I felt a bit like I was on a dating game.

Greg and I both smiled at one another before I turned away to go back to the cafeteria.

*That was weird and a bit awkward.*

I sat down at a table to wait out the lunch break, wondering if Dr. Ballard was quietly trying to play matchmaker with this body-building doctor. When the lunch break was over, I walked back into the therapy room with everyone else, but my mind was elsewhere; I couldn't stop thinking about this man I had just met.

Later that day, I ran into Dr. White while walking out to my car. My heart raced a little as we greeted each other with smiles and exchanged small talk before we left. I looked over my shoulder and saw that he was doing the same; I smiled in embarrassment before I hopped into my car.

Over the next few days, the 'chance' meetings occurred more frequently. And our casual greetings slowly turned into more meaningful talks as we would find each other in the hallway or parking lot. One day during a lunch break, I saw him sitting alone at a table eating a salad, so I sat next to him.

"So, how are you doing today?" I asked him with a smile.

"Great. How about you?"

"Great."

He smiled and looked into my blue eyes; I held the stare for a good thirty seconds before he looked away to resume eating his salad.

"Well, I have to go. So I'll see you later." I gently smiled as I got up from the table.

"Why don't you sit with me and eat lunch."

He seemed a little shocked that I was leaving so abruptly.

"I'm not really hungry."

"You don't have to eat. You can sit and talk with me while I eat."

I barely hesitated at the invitation and decided to sit back down.

Over the next few weeks, I ate lunch with Greg almost daily. And every day, he ate the same thing: a salad that he always formed into a large mountain. Lettuce and pieces of the salad always overflowed onto the table. I normally wouldn't have eaten, but I also ate a salad. Mine, however, never looked quite like his messy plate.

We talked about everything from current politics to science-related topics. He would listen intently as I talked about what I was studying in college and what my ideas were for my future. And I loved hearing him talk about his experiences as an ER doctor. It fascinated me.

I was attracted to him just as much as he seemed to be attracted to me. I eagerly anticipated talking to him every day and felt disappointed when I didn't get to see him.

Eventually, I looked forward to Guardian Hospital. I would arrive early for group and stay late so that I could run into him in the parking lot. I could tell he was always glad to see me because his eyes would light up whenever he would see me.

On the last day of my six weeks at Guardian, I was eating lunch with him, and we finally exchanged phone numbers.

"Maybe we can meet for coffee?"

\* \* \* \* \*

Two years later, Greg and I had a beautiful baby boy, and the following year, we were married. Greg helped me to feel protected and secure, which finally allowed me to work on the pressing issues of my underlying deep depression. And having a child allowed me to feel the most intense love known to mankind: the love a mother feels for her child, which is what kept me grounded and sane as I trudged through the murky waters of my memories. My son was my light home, and if I ever began to feel hopeless, his big crystal blue eyes were alone enough to bring me back again.

As for my stay at Guardian Hospital, the professionals there didn't have the "magic cure" I was searching for, but they did have Greg, and he helped me to get back on my feet and feel somewhat normal again. The new cocktail of antidepressants that Dr. Ballard prescribed me, at the highest recommended dosages, seemed to be working. A month after being discharged from Guardian, Greg talked me into enrolling in a master's degree program in counseling psychology. And, that is how I met Mark.

# Chapter 11

## The Warrior Within

*Enlightenment consists not merely in the seeing of luminous shapes and visions, but in making the darkness visible. The latter procedure is more difficult, and therefore, unpopular.*
— Carl Jung

I sighed slightly and looked up at Mark. I realized I had been rocking the chair all the time I had been talking, which gradually moved at least a foot closer to him. I stood up to move the chair back to its original position. I sat back down. I smiled slightly and said, "And that was that."

He looked at me with obvious sincerity.

"Why do you think you became so depressed in the first place?"

I shrugged my shoulders.

"I don't know."

In truth, I had thought about suicide for many years. It was during my senior year in high school when my suicidal thoughts began to grow out of control. Breaking up with my first love crushed me, so I began experimenting with different ways of hurting myself. One day, at sixteen, about six months after the breakup, I was feeling overwhelmingly depressed. I poured myself a cup of bleach and managed to gulp it. It was the most god-awful taste I'd ever experienced, and on top of that it didn't do the job. After that, it took many years for me to be able to smell bleach without cringing in disgust.

At eighteen, then a sophomore in college, I sat in my parent's bedroom closet with the barrel of my stepdad's shotgun in my mouth. There was no intention of pulling the trigger. I just wanted to see what the cold steel would feel like in my mouth. I started to sob, realizing that I was losing control of my life.

Things went from bad to worse with a second failed relationship. I had been dating my college track coach for about a year and a half, and he was twenty years older than me, but there was a strong almost magnetic connection between the two of us.

"I used to dream about you before I ever met you," he told me.

One June, his only child, nineteen, died of spinal meningitis. We never spoke again, and he became a recluse. I tried for many months to contact him, but I never got any response. It was as if he was dead himself. I didn't know why he wouldn't talk to me, and that killed me inside. Then I decided the pain had become unbearable, so I took the rat poison.

Despite all of this history, I wasn't ready to share any of it with Mark. I shrugged my shoulders when he asked me to remember.

"Well, maybe you can think about it."

*I don't want to talk to Mark about these things, at least not yet.*

"Lisa," Mark said as that first session came to an end, "you can never call after hours."

I nodded in agreement. I didn't care because I didn't want to talk to him. Only Jaime merited my attention and details. We rescheduled for the following week at 3:00 p.m.

As several months of weekly therapy sessions passed, I began to look forward to seeing him each week. I was slowly feeling comfortable enough to trust and admire Mark, and I spoke more freely about my troubled beginnings. He would always relate some philosophical or mythological story to me, an exercise for me to comprehend the ancient processes of emotions and human behavior and that what I had experienced has been going on for lifetimes, if not from the beginning of time itself.

Instead of walking head first into my trauma, he took me through a side door—the entry into knowledge.

During one session, Mark told me that I could call him whenever I needed, a reversal of his request at my first session.

"But you said I couldn't call you?"

"I know … but now you can."

His eyes twinkled as he smiled.

"Just forget that I said that and call me if you need to. It doesn't matter what time it is."

I nodded, grateful for his change of heart, I smiled and said, "Okay."

"Have you ever read any of the *Harry Potter* books?"

"Who?"

He smiled before continuing, "I think you would really enjoy them."

I drove to the bookstore after that meeting and bought the first book in the series. I began reading it that night and was finished with it by the next morning. I devoured it and left first thing in the morning to buy books two and three in the series.

Before my next session with Mark, I had read the three *Harry Potter* books.

I didn't stop to consider why he had me read the books until much later down the road.

"I guess you liked them if you've already read all three."

Light filled my eyes and voice.

"Liked them? I loved them!"

It was the classic fight between good and evil that intrigued me. But where was the therapeutic significance? I knew Mark well enough that he wouldn't have suggested a book without it holding at least some therapeutic value. But I didn't ask because I knew that in time everything would unfold.

The next summer, the fourth book in the series was released, and I was first in line to pick it up from the bookstore. I read the previous book again before beginning book four so that I could savor every last written word. I found myself daydreaming of magic and, more importantly, the power of good over evil. I saw myself as a warrior: as a protector of the weak, ready to destroy any and all evil that intruded upon my conscious realm.

Slowly, over the next several years, that feeling of power would begin to seep into my everyday life until I felt more like a warrior and less like a hopelessly vulnerable victim.

# Epilogue

The only effective way to fight one's demons is to confront them directly. It's a scary process, but in order to conquer the greatest fears, we have to do what appears at first to be the most unsettling—face them head on. For me, the demons had been long entrenched, and I had mastered the dance of evasion. Mark helped me understand why the dance with the demons had to end.

My memory of my childhood was like shattered glass. Some of the bigger pieces I could remember, but the smaller fragments were forever lost …

### ~*Easter*~

I can remember Easter when I was six years old. We were at my grandparents' house when all hell broke loose. With a beer clutched in one hand and my dad's car keys in the other, my grandma was slugging my dad repeatedly in the face. He was crying, begging her to stop, but she was relentless and continued to rampage. Eventually, he made his way outside onto the large redwood patio, and she followed close behind.

The door slammed behind them as she screamed.

"You want to fuckin' leave me?"

The look of the devil filled her drunken eyes as she glared at my dad.

"Then leave!"

But she still wouldn't give him his keys.

"Mom, please stop."

My dad, who was then in his early thirties, was crying like a deeply disappointed child. But my grandma just mockingly laughed at him and continued to hit him with his car keys clutched in her right hand.

It was late in the afternoon on Easter, plenty of time for everyone to get wasted drunk. It wasn't unusual at the holidays, or at any time the family gathered together, for a full-blown brawl to break the festive mood. But for whatever reason, this traumatic holiday stood out above the rest.

My grandma was irate because we were leaving to go to my maternal grandmother's house. My dad was the oldest of four children and was always one of the favorites in my grandma's eyes. She obviously didn't want my dad to leave, so she took his keys away from him and began hitting him.

For me, a six-year-old child, the scene was etched in my mind like a bad dream sequence of a terrible horror movie. I felt my world was spiraling out of control, and I had no where to run for cover. At least I had my cousins for comfort, three other little girls—all sisters—who were just as traumatized by this chaotic drama.

I couldn't recall where my mom was during the worst scene of this fight, but I'm sure she was there. My older brother, Troy, who was nine then, adored my dad, and I still remember seeing him on the porch steps of our grandparents' home with a mournful look on his face, helplessly wishing to come to the side of his hero. He cried just as hard as I did.

Out of nowhere, Dan, my uncle showed up, the father of my three cousins, and he slammed my grandmother into the side of the house. I thought he had killed her as her glasses fell off, and she dropped to the ground, passing out.

My grandpa tried to remove us from the scene, but my brother wouldn't budge. My cousins and I went immediately to their house, just twenty-five yards away.

The rest of the events are too obscured to recall accurately. However, I do remember later that evening, being at my other grandma's house, watching my dad cry while he was sitting on her dark wooden porch steps. Until now, I never could believe that I could really feel what a broken heart was like, especially being just six years old. I cried, sitting next to my crying dad, trying to cuddle him in my skinny arms.

## ~The Dream~

I was only six years old, and I can remember the fear I felt one night lying in almost complete darkness in my small twin bed. I had pulled my handmade Holly Hobbie bed quilt over my head to protect me from the dark formless shadows of evil monsters that lived in the darkest corners of my room, lying in wait to consume my soul.

The only light coming in was the moonlight that shined into my room, outlining the toys and furniture we had. My sister, who was six years older, slept on the other side of the room on her own twin-size bed covered with a matching Holly Hobbie quilt.

Most nights we would sleep together, hoping to ease our fears of being alone in the darkness. I'm not sure if my sister saw the same monsters, but I know she was always comforted by my warm body next to hers.

My brother had a room to himself, and he would often cry to have me come over and sleep with him. I guessed he had the same monsters in his room. But my sister always pleaded with me to stay in the room. Both would cry, begging me to sleep with them. And no matter who I chose, I would always felt the other had been betrayed. Most of the time I slept with my sister because we shared a room, and if my dad heard my brother cry for me to sleep with him, he would get yelled at.

"No son of mine is going to be a pussy! Suck it up, and be a man."

On this particular night, however, each of us was unsettlingly situated in our own beds, each equally fearful of being easy prey to the imagined monsters of the night.

A dark shadowed figure with no face was now sitting at the edge of my bed. My Holly Hobbie quilt was no longer shielding me as it had been pushed aside. I was paralyzed by fear—my eyes closed—wishing I was with my sister or brother. Goosebumps covered my small body from the coldness of the night air as the dark faceless man leaned in closer to me ...

I woke up with beads of sweat formed on my forehead and my heart pounding. I had to turn my lamp on to protect me from my formidable personal enemy of darkness. It was impossible to go back to sleep after one of those dreams because every time I would close my eyes, the fear in my dream would return. Every night I feared having the dream, but it only came to life in my unconscious mind about once a week.

## *The Pizza Parlor* ~

When I was eight years old, my mom left for a week to attend a family reunion in Wisconsin. The entire family couldn't afford to travel so far away, so we were left at home in my dad's care.

Guzzling another beer, my dad had been transformed. His hazel eyes were no longer his own after he finished off his third pitcher of Coors. He looked almost evil with his blank stare. It was almost 11:30 p.m., and I was shivering. My dad's head hit the table at the pizza parlor with a loud thump as he passed out drunk.

"I want a blanket."

I whined to my sister as I lay curled up in a ball with my head resting in her lap.

"Sssshh, I know. I'm cold, too," she whispered as she stroked my head. My brother's head was also in her lap; she rubbed our arms and legs to make us warm.

My sister, only twelve at the time, had to take control and be strong for us, but she was cold and tired, too. We knew better than to wake my dad up to ask to go home, so we sat huddled at a booth on the cold hard bench and waited.

"I'm co-co-coold," I moaned to my sister.

"I know, but you have to be quiet, so you don't wake Dad up, and we'll go home soon," she said as she rubbed her hands faster on my arms and legs. "Put your legs in your shirt."

My dad picked his head up from the table and glared at me.

"You want me to give you something to cry about, you little pussy?"

I shook my head no, and then buried my face in my sister's lap. My brother and I clutched on to her tighter.

"I want Mom!" my brother cried.

"Oh, you want your mommy," my dad said mockingly.

"You must be a fuckin' little baby to want your mommy. You fuckin' pussy."

He tipped back his mug of beer to finish off its contents before passing out again.

At 1:00 a.m., the owner of the pizza parlor came up to our table.

"Excuse me, sir. You've got to wake up. We're closing the pizza parlor."

My dad picked his head up from the table and snarled at the owner.

"What?"

"We're closing."

"What the fuck! You're kickin' me and my fuckin' babies out of here?"

The man didn't respond. He just turned and walked away.

"Let's get the fuck out of this place. We're not welcome here anymore," he yelled in the direction of the owner. He stumbled a little as he got out of the booth and began walking to the car.

"Come on, we're going," Lori whispered to us as she gathered us. She strained from the weight of my body, carrying me to the car.

"What the fuck do you think you're doing? She's too fuckin' old to be carried. Put her down," my dad roared.

"But she's tired and cold," my sister pleaded.

He glared at her, daring her to disobey him. Unaffected, she took a few more steps before putting me down. I whined and cried, wanting her to pick me back up. I was so tired. The crisp cold night air did nothing to make me feel better. I plopped down in the parking lot and started crying. My sister and brother immediately came to my side to get me up and to the car as fast as possible before my dad noticed. But it was too late.

"What the fuck, you little pussy? Get your little ass up off the ground before I really give you something to cry about."

He screamed, which only make me cry harder, so I had to force the tears back by holding my breath. Otherwise, I'd risk being hit.

I stood up, holding my sister's left hand as she put me into our white-and-blue El Camino. My dad didn't even wait for us to buckle our seat belts before he peeled away from the lot with the tires squealing.

On the quiet country road, driving like a bat out of hell, my dad swerved back and forth over the road divider. Near our house, there was a railroad crossing, and the lights were flashing and the crossarms lowered.

"We can make it."

My dad accelerated to race the train. We were beating the train by only twenty feet when we came to the blinking red lights and lowered crossarms, but instead of stopping like we were supposed to, he floored the accelerator. Swerving through the lowered arms, the train's ear-piercing horn blared as its headlight illuminated the entire car. All of us screamed for dad to stop. Now, it seems a miracle that we made it through safely. The piercing horn blast of the train still reverberates in my memory.

* * * *

These stories are just a small sample of what I experienced as a child, trying to grow up in an abusive environment. As tempting as it is to catalogue these stories—which I'm sure reflect in some form and variation the experiences and details of countless hundreds of thousands of individuals, the purpose here was not merely to recount the litany of those horrifying stories. Rather, it is to show that there are great, untapped reservoirs of love out there, and no matter how dreadful our life experiences seem at times, each of us—sometimes alone and sometimes with the guidance of a counselor, advocate, teacher, or mentor—can begin to find the capacity to rise above the dread, confront the negativity, and repudiate those internalized forces that threaten our will and our potential for getting the stability each of us so desperately craves. Finally, I was willing to let people into my life and heart and to begin feeling my way for that path that would eventually lead me to recovery and a brighter, much enlightened personal perspective.

It was Jaime's love and compassion that led me to her mentor, Mark. And it was Mark who was able to catch me in the middle of my freefall. Mark succeeded not only in catching me but also in teaching me to navigate the turbulence and bumps of our individual flights through life.

Mark helped me sort through my memories and showed me, through his love and compassion, how to find goodness in myself. He taught me that my childhood fear was no longer real, and that I was strong and completely capable of conquering evil no matter its form. He helped me understand that my internal hate was just a mask of the anger locked inside me.

I could now see that negative, evil people were really the weak ones. And that pity—not fear—was the appropriate emotion. Unshackled from the prison of victimhood, I was clearly empowered. However, instead of misusing power and risking become a negative evil person, I had decided that I, too, could follow Mark's example.

I was a client of Mark's for a little more than eight years until he eventually retired. What I learned and gained from him during those years was invaluable, and no one can take it away from me because it's forever locked in my heart and mind.

He gave me the best gift of all. He taught me to know and experience the power to love, strong enough to manage and overcome any and every obstacle. I had learned that love can obliterate despair—the omnipresent light in darkness.

After being imprisoned for so long by the deepest and darkest of depression, I feared that it would only be a matter of time before I was once again taken hostage and destroyed by it. I was doing okay, but what about five or even ten years from now? I knew I couldn't survive through that extreme darkness again.

It seems like I woke up one day, and the world didn't seem so dark. I'm not saying that depressing thoughts don't creep into my mind now and then—because they do—but I've also learned that it's just a normal part of life. Most importantly, I understand that the part of myself I feared losing most was the part holding me back from coming to a healthy, peaceful point in my life. That part was false. It really wasn't a part of who I am.

I feel like I have something important to share with the world, and that's why I'm still here today. Everybody experiences hardship in many forms and many degrees, and demographics do not dictate those experiences. Regardless of economic, social, and cultural circumstances, the fact remains that so many children are physically and mentally beaten until their spirits are broken, and many face exceedingly difficult lives of trying to regain what they lost as children in terms of the inner strength. In the extreme, they give up on love and life or at least give up on the hope that there are people in the world who may truly care about them.

Today I live for what I can control in any given day and deal with what I can't control. I wake up in the morning with one goal and that is to spread love to at least one person. It might be to one of my children, my husband, a family member, a close friend, a casual or professional acquaintance, or a stranger. Whomever the recipient, it doesn't really matter as long as my intention is to spread love.

And, sometimes simple acts of kindness can alter the course of another person's life in unforeseen ways.

A few months ago, I was in a drive-through line at a local coffee shop, and I was feeling depressed and burdened by the natural weight of life. I doubted what I had been studying and learning about over the last year, which was the foundation of my newfound strength. I had been learning about the infinite love of the universe, that we are constantly surrounded by a pure love. People call it many things: God, Allah, Krishna, Buddha, etc. Whatever any of us want to call it, one truth remains: there is an energy of love just like there is an energy of negativity pulsating through the entire planet.

I challenged the Universe or God. Aloud, while still in my car, I said, "If all that I'm learning is true, then give me a sign—big or small—I don't care. I'm tired, and I'm going to give up if I don't get a sign soon."

I felt pleased with my request. I smugly thought to myself that nothing would happen and it would all be over.

I continued to wait maybe two more minutes before I pulled up to the drive-through window. I rolled my window down and handed my money out to the cashier, but she didn't take it.

She smiled and said, "The car in front of you just paid for your coffee."

With a look of confusion on my face, I tried to give her the money again.

Still not taking my money, she shook her head and repeated, "The woman in front of you paid for your coffee."

My eyes lit up as I began to comprehend the enormity of what just happened.

"She did?"

"Yeah," she said, smiling.

As she handed me coffee for myself and two hot chocolates for my sons, she added, "She told me to tell you that a grandmother bought you a coffee."

The woman in front of me did one small kind act for a stranger, but it was transforming for me. She solidified all that I had been studying with the tremendous focus of a student who was going to ace the final exam for sure. From that moment on, I never doubted that God's love is real. Something or someone in the universe heard my cry for help and immediately gave me what I needed: a small tangential piece of proof that something much greater than me is undoubtedly present in an unseen world, and it's beautiful—full of love, compassion, and peace.

Once I began to open my heart to the love and energy of God, I noticed miracles occurring around me: some small and some large.

One spring morning in 2006, I woke to find that, once again, I was beginning to feel smothered by darkness. The heaviness of life was stacking up onto my shoulders, and my knees felt weakened as if they were ready to buckle. Tears filled my eyes as I drove my red Honda Element into town.

Feeling desperate, I once again sent out a mental plea to God: *If you really are there then give me a sign.*

I went to the post office to check my mail. Once I parked, I drew a deep breath and left my car, not expecting to receive a sign now or ever for that matter. It was early in the spring, so the morning air was still crisp against my face. With the tiny key in hand, I took only a few steps before reaching the mailbox.

A large amount of mail had been stuffed into the tiny metal box.

*The postal workers probably hate me because I never check my mail.*

An oversized envelope that had been folded gave me an especially difficult time. Junk mail. I returned to my car, but before I opened the door, I noticed something on the ground sitting right at the toe of my right shoe.

My heart skipped a beat because I knew immediately this was the sign that I had asked for just moments earlier. With a knowing smile but with a tinge of disbelief, I bent down to pick up a shiny gold-looking coin upon which an angel kneeling with her arms folded in prayer had been engraved. I grasped the coin tightly, hoping that there was no one around who would want to reclaim the lost coin.

However, I was alone on what normally is a busy street. This particular morning—a weekend day—there were no cars, no people. The only sound was the usual morning song of birds. I examined the coin, expecting to find some evidence to discredit what had just happened, but nothing seemed apparent. Now feeling not just happy but joyful, I settled into my red Honda Element, still clasping tightly my newly found largesse.

The serendipity of the moment amused me, and I laughed.

*I can't believe that this has just happened again!*

Aloud, I said, "Thank you for making me feel so special."

No longer chilled in the morning air, I felt reassured as a warm current of energy flowed though my body and a single tear of happiness escaped from my right eye and fell onto my hand.

Several miraculous things happened to me in the following year. It didn't matter where I was or what I was doing. If I put a heartfelt cry out into the universe I would always receive some response in physical form—often seemingly inconspicuous or trivial. That warm current always followed, a gracious punctuation mark to the acceptance of a small gift.

The gifts are important. I have a solid sense of purpose, and for the first time, it feels good to be alive. I feel blessed to be standing with my feet so firmly on the ground. My strength comes from many sources of love, but perhaps the most amazing is that love doesn't necessarily have to come from another person. I've learned to see and feel the love of the universe pulsating around me, often manifested in small strokes of grace and gifts.

There are occasional moments and times when my inner sense of strength is challenged. Depression still tries to seep back into my mind, but I also have learned to deflect it with knowledge, a great weapon in my personal arsenal. It starts with a remarkably simple acknowledgment—there is the capacity to generate love and enlightenment in our individual souls, and because of that capacity, I know I will never again stand in darkness.

## About the Author

**Lisa White** is a Marriage and Family Therapist practicing psychotherapy in Northern California. She has worked with troubled youth and addicts for seven years. She lives happily in a small town in Northern California, with her husband and two young children.

www.ingramcontent.com/pod-product-compliance
Ingram Content Group UK Ltd.
Pitfield, Milton Keynes, MK11 3LW, UK
UKHW041957230426
12048UKWH00008B/392